Founda... OD

Day 1: Jes...
is the Liv...

...es faced
...eople
Jesus
...way that

FRAMEWORKS

We need the right foundations for any building work. Jesus Himself told a story about two people building houses: one had good foundations on a rock and the other had no proper foundations on the sand. The foundations made all the difference between happiness and disaster.

Without solid foundations we cannot build a house.

> Read that story from Jesus. Read Matthew 7:13-27.
> What strikes you about that teaching?
> If Jesus is telling us how to lay *the* right foundations, then what are the foundations that He is describing?

Following the commands of Jesus is where all theology and life must begin. Theology is not for the intellectually gifted or those who like studying old books. Theology is the "study of God" and He has walked among us to tell us how to live.

He told us to follow Him and we will freely receive life, forgiveness, cleansing and wisdom, without money and without price. When we fall, He will help us to get back up and carry on following Him, over and over again. Aspects of the foundations of theology have shifted at different times in history, around the world.

In the early years after the apostles a big part of the foundation was what we call the Old Testament. In later years Church life and authority played a bigger role but in parts of the world philosophy from people who never followed Jesus was introduced into the foundations.

We need to be so careful about our foundations in life and theology. How we think shapes how we live and feel. If our thinking is twisted then our emotions, perceptions and actions will all be twisted too.

They thought that Jesus is divine – in some sense. They thought that He could not be as perfectly divine as the Father because Jesus has been so involved in this messy physical world.

They had allowed outside philosophy into their theology.

They allowed pagan assumptions into their foundations.

So, they thought that perhaps He was a kind of Divine Creature – the first and greatest creature, made by the Father before the universe began.

They thought that there was a bigger and better kind of "divinity" above and beyond Jesus – even though Jesus is the best that this world can handle.

So, church leaders from all over the world – Europe, Asia and Africa – got together to think of a way of expressing the ancient faith of the Bible.

They created the Nicene Creed, which has become the standard of all church teaching ever since!

The original Nicene Creed from 325 AD.

We believe in one God:

The Father Almighty, Maker of all things visible and invisible;

And in one Lord Jesus Christ, the Son of God, begotten of the Father the only-begotten; that is, of the essence of the Father, **God of God, Light of Light, very God of very God**, begotten, not made, being of one substance with the Father; by whom all things were made both in heaven and on earth; who for us human beings, and for our salvation, came down and was incarnate and was made human; He suffered, and the third day He rose again, ascended into heaven; from there He shall come to judge the living and the dead.

And in the Holy Spirit.

But those who say: 'There was a time when He was not'... — they are condemned by the holy catholic and apostolic Church.

In the modern age there has been perhaps the biggest change of all, from the study of **theology** to the study of "religion".

Colleges that used to offer serious theology courses now offer courses in "the study of religion".

This is a huge shift from the study of the Living God Himself to the study of what human beings think about religion or their gods.

Instead of studying the Living God there was a general conclusion, especially in the Western world, that it was impossible to say anything for sure about "God" – and so it was considered to be much safer to just study "religion", what **human beings** think or believe about God, gods or ultimate reality.

This huge change shows up in the study of the Bible also. From seeing the Biblical text as a unique, almost mystical text through which the Living God speaks the unchanging teaching of the Church... the study of the Bible has shifted to trying to understand or reconstruct what the **human** authors were thinking, believing or trying to say.

There may be good reasons for studying human religion or investigating the ancient world or trying to understand the psychology or literary techniques of ancient Biblical writers. However, none of these activities are **theology** – in the sense that local churches have always meant.

In this month we are going to see why Jesus Himself is the rock-solid foundation of theology. When we say that, we mean that the central teaching of the Church down the ages is that Jesus is Himself the Living God. Jesus did not come to tell us **about** a God somewhere else, but rather He acts and speaks as the LORD God Himself. If **that** is true, then all study of God must be the study of Jesus.

If we think there is anything **other** than Jesus at the centre of theology then it must be because we are not sure that He really **is** the Living God.

In the end, this whole month we are going to state and try to appreciate that Jesus is God.

Hardly anyone really believes that.

Foundations

Day 2: Don't try to get behind Jesus

FRAMEWORKS

If we are going to live and think as Church people should, then we must keep our hearts and minds fixed on Jesus of Nazareth.

This sounds so obvious that it shouldn't need to be said, but in fact there are so many temptations, clever and stupid, to look for answers elsewhere.

One of the common challenges is to assume that there is some bigger and deeper reality of God that is above and beyond Jesus. If we go down this dead-end then we are always looking to see what is going on over Jesus' shoulder!

Sometimes people look at Jesus but imagine that He is simply the façade for a deeper reality. They think that the idea of "God" or "spirituality" cannot be confined in just one historical person.

The idea is that we can go beyond Jesus to something bigger, more universal. I have even heard people say things like "I used to be focussed on Jesus but now I've matured beyond that to something bigger, to a bigger view of God".

> Read Colossians 2:4-10. Paul wrote to this local Church because they seemed to think that they needed other things alongside of Jesus in order to get the full picture of reality. They seemed to think knowledge of angels, spirituality and religion were all necessary to live a full and fruitful life.
>
> As you read these verses, take time to appreciate how big this view of Jesus is. Note down the things that strike you – even if you can't quite cope with it yet!

There are several popular modern authors who think that Jesus is nothing more than a "version" of God that was packaged to certain people at a particular time... BUT, there are other ways of packaging God to different people at other times!

GETTING TO THE MOST BASIC REALITY

Let's think a bit more about the Nicene Creed and the full divinity of Jesus.

Arius was a Berber church leader from north Africa, born in 256. He lived a long and controversial life, right down to 336.

North Africa was the heart of Church doctrine for the first 500 years of Church history after the apostles. A great church leader called Tertullian from a hundred years earlier had invented the word "trinity" to express the Bible's ancient teaching about the eternal divine nature. A century after Arius, another Berber called Augustine would shape Western Church life right down to the present day!

So, we have high expectations when we study north African theologians! However, Arius was dangerous because his starting point was Greek philosophy rather than Jesus Himself.

Arius had a clear idea of what God is, an idea that he had received from the pagan philosophy of the Greeks. This alien way of imagining God was stronger to Arius than anything he could see in Jesus Christ.

Arius always thought that Jesus was not "the real thing", but only a lesser version of the full deity of the Father.

Arius wrote a book called "The Feast" in which he set out his own view of God.

In this quotation from Arius' book, take time to note down how Arius' view of Jesus is very different to what the Bible and the Church teach.

God Himself, as he really is, is inexpressible to all.
He alone has no equal, no one similar and no one of the same glory.
We call him unborn, in contrast to him who by nature is born [Jesus].
We praise him as without beginning in contrast to him who has a beginning [Jesus].
We worship him as timeless, in contrast to him who in time has come to exist [Jesus].
He who is without beginning made the Son a beginning of created things.
He produced him as a son for himself by begetting him.
Jesus has none of the distinct characteristics of God's own being
For he is not equal to, nor is he of the same being as the Father...
The Father is invisible both to things which were made through the Son, and also to the Son himself...
As far as their glories, one is infinitely more glorious than the other.
The Father in his nature is a foreigner to the Son, because he exists without beginning...
Jesus, not being [eternal] came into existence by the Father's will.

[We have used the name of Jesus rather than just Son in this quotation to focus our thoughts on what Arius is saying.]

If we fall into this way of thinking then we are always trying to see above and beyond Jesus, as if He were just a lower level of God or a limited perspective about God.

The problem is that we might think we already know what God is like before we ever think about Jesus, before we ever read about Jesus.

If we are already convinced that God cannot be very physical or earthly, then we will have a problem with Jesus. If we already believe that God is beyond history or even "beyond words" then we will struggle with the words of Jesus and the fact that He is Himself called The Word.

Jesus clearly does not fit into most of the ideas about God that human philosophy and human religion have developed. He is too physical for most of them and He is too exclusive for others. He seems to be both impossibly arrogant on the one hand, when He says that all the ancient Scriptures are talking about Him and that Moses and Abraham met Him. Yet, on the other hand, He is completely humble in serving the lowliest people, washing their feet and embracing the outcasts.

Jesus will always disturb and outrage human ideas about God, religion and the universe.

We need to take this seriously because we too will often be tempted to explain Him away or limit what the Bible says about Him.

If Jesus does not upset us, enrage us and disturb us we have not listened to Him or seen Him properly. Yes, we should also fall in love with Him and worship Him, but He will always be turning over the tables that we have neatly arranged in our "temples".

This is why the Bible, and Jesus, says "let those who have ears to hear, listen..."

Foundations

Day 3: Is Jesus really the foundation for our Church life?

FRAMEWORKS

Over the years I have often asked church leaders if Jesus is their foundation, if Jesus is the centre of their theology and Church life. Most of the time they give a very strong "Yes!"

It seems obvious. We sing songs about Jesus, telling Him how much we love Him and that He means more to us than anything in the world; we listen to worship music that states that Jesus is the highest Name, the LORD over all the heavens and the earth, the Beginning and the End, the First and the Last.

Yet, when we have done all those things, it is no guarantee that we will really believe all our songs in daily life and thought.

The follow up questions might be these: what does your Church life look like? What gets the time and money? What are people encouraged to do? What is the teaching about?

In practice it seems that "God", mission and the Bible are often the centre, rather than Jesus. That sounds very controversial because surely all of those things are good things. Surely they **should** be at the centre of all we do in Church and how we think! In one sense, yes, but if any of these things are the foundation rather than Jesus then things go wrong.

It is **God**-centred people who kill Christians all over the world today.
It is **mission**-centred people who have been caught up in some of the most terrible abuse.
It was **Bible**-centred people who killed Jesus.

Mission divorced from Jesus is dangerous.

In recent years we have heard so many stories about charity workers abusing the very people they were supposed to help. History tells us that the high-minded revolutionaries are tomorrow's tyrants.

THE DANGER OF MAKING THE BIBLE, GOD OR MISSION AS OUR FOUNDATION

The **Bible** is only interesting or powerful because it is about Jesus.

It is the Word of God only because it is filled with Jesus.

Jesus is Himself the eternal Word of God – and the Bible shares that reality only because it is about Him.

When the Bible is studied with great care and diligence **without** meeting Jesus on every page, it leads people to be the greatest enemies of Jesus.

Mission is only ever genuinely revolutionary and transformative when it introduces people to Jesus.

Jesus is not like self-help gurus who give some principles of improvement for us to work on or guide us how to help ourselves.

Jesus is the Great High Priest of the cosmos, who holds all things together; He is the Divine Saviour who plunged down to the depths of Hell on the Cross to go as far away from God as it is possible to go... in order to be able to rescue every last one of us.

Mission that doesn't have **that** big picture in mind tends to treat human beings far cheaper than they are. If we think the way to fix people is **only** by giving them more food and money, then we do not see them the way that Jesus sees them.

Jesus thought human beings needed something as precious as the very blood of God to rescue them.

Talk about **God** that is not talk about Jesus from start to finish is delusional and dangerous.

It is delusional because Jesus Himself claimed that nobody knows anything about God other than Him: He alone is the visible form of the invisible God.

As Peter put it in the first chapter of his letter – **Because of Jesus we believe in God.**

Trying to talk about a generic God is meaningless and dangerous.

What good would it have been for Elijah and the prophets of Baal to find common ground in a shared theism... or for Paul to see "belief in god" as a step in the right direction for the worshippers of Diana at Ephesus?

Religion without Jesus drains life away. It can easily be turned to political and economic corruption.

John 5:39-40 – "You study the Scriptures diligently because you think that in **them** you have eternal life. These are the very Scriptures that testify about me yet you refuse to come to me to have life."

Social care outside of Church is always at best partial.

We are most often known as "Christians" – a title that was first given to us at Antioch, according to Acts 11:26. That seems to mean the pagan world perceived the apostolic churches to be obsessed with Christ Jesus – and yet is that the sort of title we would earn today? What are the titles that are most often given to us today...? Do people normally refer to us as the Jesus-people? Perhaps people think we go on about God, the Bible, "religion", "public morality", "busy-bodies" and perhaps mission in the sense of "trying to do some social good".

Speaking about Jesus is disruptive and troublesome. It is much easier to speak about moral issues or "God" or do studies about "what the Bible teaches".

Mission that is not Jesus-centred is in the end cynical and patronising... because it tries to palm people off with far less than they deserve; it treats human beings as if we were not worth the life of God.

Talk about God that is not talk about Jesus is dangerous because as Marx and many other social commentators say – god and religion are very dangerous tools for manipulation and control.
When we are trying to do "religion" but we are no longer talking about Jesus... we are walking onto very dangerous ground that has a long history of darkness, abuse and cynicism.

> Remember what Jesus said to the Bible-centred Pharisees in John 5:39-47. If you have time read the whole chapter. This chapter shows what happens when people have a very different idea about God in their minds when they meet Jesus.
>
> John 5:39-47 has some very deep truth about the Bible. What are the main things that Jesus states about the ancient Scriptures? Remember that Jesus is speaking about the Old Testament in this speech. Do Jesus words fit with your own view of the Old Testament? Could Moses really have written about a man who lived 1500 years later?

Bible study must always begin with the question: what does this teach me about Jesus? Some may find that question too naïve or simplistic, but it seems to be the question the Bible wants us to ask.

Foundations

Day 4: No one has ever seen God

FRAMEWORKS

Think about that glorious opening section of John's biography of Jesus. We are used to biographies that begin with the parents or even grandparents, but when it comes to Jesus John begins before the universe began. Jesus' family tree takes us to eternal realms and infinite ages.

> Read John 1:1-18 and try to make a list of all the extraordinary facts in Jesus background.
>
> What are His qualifications for revealing the truth about God?
>
> Take time to carefully consider this question because it is critical to the foundations we are laying.

There was a man called Justin Martyr in the second century who was searching for the truth in philosophy. One day he met an elderly Christian man by the seaside, and they began to chat. Justin provided a philosopher's idea of God and the other man asked him how he could know such a thing. If nobody has ever seen God and our minds are inadequate to grasp the infinite life of God... then none of us know what we are talking about. All human talk about God is just fantasy and foolishness.

However, Justin Martyr was shown that Jesus was spoken about by the most ancient prophets and He alone has seen and understood the Living God, because He is Himself the Eternal God with His Father and the Spirit.

The point is powerful. John 1:18 tells us clearly what we all know: nobody on earth has ever seen the Most High God at any time; nobody has seen the Father's face. People have met Jesus, God the Son since the world began, even before He became a human being but nobody has ever been able to find their own way to seeing God the Father.

However, nearly everybody has an opinion about "God"! Everybody seems to know things about God – yet nobody has ever seen Him. Nobody knows what they are talking about!

JESUS DISPLAYS THE INVISIBLE FATHER

Irenaeus was one of the great church leaders of the 2nd century, based in Lyons.

In his amazing work "Against Heresies" he explains how Jesus has always been revealing the Father, in the Old Testament just as much as the New Testament times.

"Clearly the Father is indeed invisible, of whom also the Lord said, "No one has seen God at any time."

But His Word, as He Himself willed it and for the benefit of those who beheld it, did show the Father's brightness and explained His purposes—as also the Lord said, "The only begotten God, which is in the bosom of the Father, He has declared [Him]."

And, He Himself also interprets the Word of the Father as being rich and great.

He appeared not only in one figure or in one character to those who saw Him, but according to whatever purpose or effect He was aiming for in His plan of salvation.

CHRIST IS THE TRUE INTERPRETER OF THE LIVING GOD

One of the most brilliant Church leaders of all history was a man called Ambrose, the Bishop of Milan. Many of the great songs and patterns of Christian worship find their roots in his work at Milan.

He also wanted to make it clear that only Jesus can explain the Godhead – the nature of God Himself.

For Christ is the interpreter of the Godhead, because "no one has at any time seen God, except the only begotten Son, who is in the bosom of the Father, He has revealed him."

There are many things even here on earth that are extremely difficult to see. Think about atoms and subatomic particles; forms of light beyond our visible range; sound vibrations in the air; tiny creatures that live on our bodies or in our gut; fish that live in the darkness of the ocean depths.

If it is so hard to see even things that are right within our grasp on this planet, how far more difficult it is to see creatures that live in realms beyond our reach or perception – like angels or "spirits". We don't have reliable ways to see or understand any such creatures. So, it is fantastically impossible for us to even imagine seeing the Infinite and Eternal God!

People assume they know at least **some** things about God. Often they imagine that He is some kind of "old man in the sky" or some kind of invisible cloud of good will or a "supreme being without limits". When people wonder if **this** "God" really exists, they are thinking of Him as something like an animal or big planet that exists somewhere in the universe – and it might be possible to get "evidence" of this "thing" as it moves around!

It is hard enough to scientifically examine many things in the heavens and the earth, but what possible "scientific" tools could there be to examine the Infinite and Eternal God who is described as holding the entire universe in His hands?

I had a watershed moment when I was still a teenager. I had all kinds of ideas about God and some strong opinions on the subject. I assumed that God must fit in with the best human logic and the highest human ideas about what is good. I was arguing with a Christian friend and he simply stopped me and said, "you must deal with the real God, not the one you would like or imagine."

It stopped me dead. It had never occurred to me that the real God might not be what I wanted Him to be! He might be many things I didn't want Him to be...

Deal with the real. Nobody has ever seen God – and unless that God made Himself known we couldn't know anything at all about God. That seems to be one of the foundational truths in the Bible. Everybody **thinks** they know things about God... but only Jesus really knows what He is talking about.

Foundations

Day 5: Philosophers have not seen God

FRAMEWORKS

Nearly everybody assumes that philosophy can find things out about God, whether in the Greek or Hindu traditions. Some of the most brilliant human minds have thought their way to one god, many gods or even no gods at all. The knowledge of "God" is thought of as almost "common sense" that a bit of serious thinking will deliver!

Theistic schools of Hinduism use their philosophy to define God as is "the sum of all noble attributes—omniscient, omnipotent, omnipresent, and all merciful."

Shankara who lived in the 8th century may have been the most brilliant philosopher to have ever lived. He defined "ultimate reality" as "without parts or attributes".

Even godly Christians fall into this: the Westminster Confession begins its definition of God with "There is but one only, living, and true God, who is infinite in being and perfection, a most pure spirit, invisible, without body, parts, or passions; immutable, immense, eternal, incomprehensible, almighty, most wise, most holy, most free, most absolute…"

When faced with people who reject Jesus and do not respect the Bible there is a strong temptation to find some **other** path to God, a path that non-Christians might accept or recognise.

> Read carefully 1 Corinthians 1:17-31. Paul gives a choice between Greek philosophy on the one hand and the demand for displays of power on the other – but neither of these ways of discovering God are looking at Jesus who dies in weakness, looking so foolish to the surrounding world. Next, turn the page and look at 1 Corinthians 2:6-16. Is it possible to use human wisdom [which is what philosophy is] to show of the Living God?
>
> How can we know the mind of God if it is impossible to comprehend?
>
> What are the roles of Jesus Christ and the Holy Spirit in knowing the Living God?

TRINITY OR THEISM?

The first article of the 39 articles of the Church of England starts off as if it were going to use philosophy to know God but abandons that as a bad idea and just embraces the Trinity instead!

"There is but one living and true God, everlasting, without body, parts, or passions; of infinite power, wisdom, and goodness; the Maker, and Preserver of all things both visible and invisible. And in unity of this Godhead there be three Persons, of one substance, power, and eternity; the Father, the Son, and the Holy Ghost."

Monotheistic philosophers argue that it is logical for there to be only one all-powerful god, because it would be illogical to have more than one all-powerful god. The universe isn't big enough for two Almighty gods!

Yet, polytheistic philosophers think it is perfectly logical to have many very powerful gods – gods who are not everlasting gods who have children and successors. Roman, Greek and Nordic religious traditions have all those colourful and complex gods who vie with one another, embody natural forces and even choose lovers.

Are these gods any less "logical" than the lonely absolute being with no parts – high on attributes but low on personality?

Isaiah 64:4-7 says that the Living God gladly comes to the help of all those who wait for Him, who remember His ways.

He is not hiding; He is easy to know through Jesus.

"Since ancient times no one has heard, no ear has perceived, no eye has seen any God besides you, who acts on behalf of those who wait for Him. You come to the help of those who gladly do right, who remember your ways. But when we continued to sin against them, you were angry. How then can we be saved? All of us have become like one who is unclean, and all our righteous acts are like filthy rags; we all shrivel up like a leaf, and like the wind our sins sweep us away. No one calls on your name or strives to lay hold of you; for you have hidden your face from us and have given us over to our sins."

Religious philosophy has been one of the most powerful and persuasive alternatives to Jesus and the Bible. The Bible is not very positive about the power of the human mind to discover the Living God.

The apostle Paul quoted Isaiah 29:14 in his first chapter, and it is useful to see why.

Religious philosophy assumes it is very clever and that the problem of knowing God is a problem that we are capable of solving. The assumption is that God has hidden Himself in some way – perhaps simply by being very complicated or big, very far away or just invisible. So, it is down to us to deal with this problem of finding God and our philosophy is smart enough to do it.

However, listen to the words of Isaiah 29:13-16

The Lord says: "These people come near to me with their mouth and honour me with their lips, but their hearts are far from me. Their worship of me is based on merely human rules they have been taught. Therefore, once more I will astound these people with wonder upon wonder; the wisdom of the wise will perish, the intelligence of the intelligent will vanish. Woe to those who go to great depths to hide their plans from the Lord, who do their work in darkness and think, "Who sees us? Who will know?" You turn things upside down, as if the potter were thought to be like the clay! Shall what is formed say to the one who formed it, "You did not make me"? Can the pot say to the potter, "You know nothing"?

The Living God is not the one who is hiding. He looks at human beings and sees that although we **talk** about God, our hearts are messed up and corrupt, full of selfishness and deceitful desires. We think that this inner mess is hidden and under control, but we are utterly exposed to the Living God – who is not far away or hiding at all. The Father sends His Son in the power of the Spirit to hold everything together and give light & life to all humanity.

Religious philosophy treats God as needing help, as if He knows nothing – but we need to face up to the fact that it is we human beings who are ignorant, blind and corrupt.

Foundations

Day 6: Religious leaders have not seen God

FRAMEWORKS

Older generations in the Western world often have a very low view of religion.

Religion was what the Enlightenment worked so hard to get rid of. Religion was portrayed as mumbo jumbo, superstition, bowing and scraping, blind faith, abuse of authority, repressive rules and oppressive dogmas.

In some forms of the post-Enlightenment re-telling of human history, alongside **biological** evolution from a single cell right up to human beings, there was a **religious** evolution from a kind of animism that worshipped natural objects and phenomena, through to polytheism which saw all these natural forces concentrated in specific diverse deities, to monotheism which advanced further with the idea of concentrating all these natural forces in just one mega god, until finally the final stage of evolution was the liberating and empowering realisation that there are only natural forces that can be full understood in their own terms.

Naturally, these very Euro-centric systems of "evolution" tended to place traditional African religion at the single-celled stage, Hindu religions generally at the invertebrate stage, Islam and Judaism at the vertebrate stage, domesticated Western Christianity was perhaps the ape stage and finally secular atheism or rationalist deism was the pinnacle of evolution.

However, in the 21st centre, plenty of people are rediscovering the comfort and security of religion. The rationalist vision of a perfect world without religion [think here of John Lennon's song *Imagine*] has not appeared. The 20th century was the age when the non-religious regimes had a chance to lead the nations of the world, but never before was there so much violent death, war, starvation and destruction.

Yet, for many younger people in the 21st century the deepest problem is the lack of meaning and purpose.

A FAITH FOR THIS ONE WORLD?

Lesslie Newbiggin's brilliant book with this title looks at Jesus as the answer to the world's religions. At the end of chapter 2 he writes:

"Can we of the twentieth century still believe that this faith, centred in the Name of *one* of the world's great religious figures, can be the universal faith for mankind? If we do so believe, are we merely betraying our inability to rise above the limitations of our own tradition? I answer that question by putting another: when we look for a universal faith for mankind, what are we expecting to find? Are we expecting to find something so wholly free from the taint of locality that it has already occurred to everybody everywhere? Obviously not…

What then are we seeking? Surely what we seek is a harmony of wills in which our several wills without being destroyed are redeemed from their natural egotism and brought into cooperation. We seek reconciliation, and we know that without it we shall certainly destroy one another. But reconciliation can only come from a new birth of love in men's hearts, and love cannot be begotten out of fear. The very reiteration of our need for unity, and of the appalling horrors that will attend our failure to find it, strengthens all those self-regarding elements which are the enemy of love. Only love can beget love. But how shall love be found? It is not in man. We must ask it of God. But how shall God show his love if not by deeds? And if they are deeds, they have a date and place. Is it irrational then to look to particular and local events as the possible source of a universal faith? Rather, it would surely be irrational to refuse so to look…

How can we find a peace which does not become mere appeasement and a righteousness that does not become self-righteousness? Only at the place where there is a holy forgiveness, which means the forgiveness of God against whom men have sinned and who is our judge. The place where righteousness and peace have kissed each other must be provided by God who alone can forgive sin. That place must be somewhere, for forgiveness is an act that must have a date and place...

We have talked about man's quest for unity. All that I have said leads simply to this point: man cannot find it, God must give it. Like Job and his friends, we have to stop talking and listen because God has spoken. The roles are suddenly reversed. When you pick up a Bible in the midst of a discussion such as we have had, it is as though you have suddenly to turn around and face the other way. The questions you were asking die on your lips. For you realize that you are now the one who is questioned. The programme is after all not in your hands but in those of another, and the question is, are you ready for all that it involves? Not that you are swept off your feet; certainly not. You are required to stand and answer. But it is a much more tremendous question even than you had realized. It is not just a matter of life and death; it is a message from beyond death. The dying and rising of Jesus constitutes an event beside which even the future existence of human civilization is a secondary question. The Christian claim is that that event has to be announced to the whole world as the one secret of reconciliation first between man and his Maker and second between man and man."

If in the end there are only natural forces without any awareness of human beings, then there is no meaning "out there": there is only the personal meaning that we give to our own lives. This is a very heavy burden for young people to bear! To assign meaning to the world, the universe, history and your own life, whilst also trying to invent an identity that you find plausible... it is all too much for ordinary human beings.

So, it is quite understandable that younger generations are reaching for the comfort and security of religion.

Religions carry traditions that have been passed on for hundreds or even thousands of years. Religion is human philosophy dressed in rituals, festivals, buildings, ancient traditions, sacred places, taboos, mystical authority and complex texts. Every religion carries plenty of human wisdom accumulated down the generations – about home and family, marriage and sex, loyalty and honour, money and possessions, bravery and compassion, community and kingdom. Parts of the religions sound like they are borrowed from the Bible, whilst other parts most definitely do not!

Religion makes us feel that we are in touch with God or "the divine" or "ultimate reality". When we are surrounded by many people all following a strong, colourful and ancient religious tradition, it feels like we have found the answer. The rituals and festivals give an order to our lives, make us feel right and give a sense of meaning. However, the Bible is filled with strong warnings against religion. Religion does not know the Living God. It is lifeless but seductive.

> The Bible deals with human religions at various points. Read some or all of these Scriptures to get a sense of how the LORD Jesus looks at religion.
>
> Numbers 33:50-53; Deut 7:1-6 Deut 12:1-4; Deut 29:16-18; Deut 32:15-21; 1 Kings 18; Isaiah 41:21-24; Isaiah 44:6-26; Jeremiah 16:19-21.

The Word of God does not see human religions as alternative sources of divine revelation in any way. In fact, within the Bible, the Word of God uniformly rejects every religion it encounters! No matter how ancient, clever, beautiful, powerful or serious a religion is, no religion can replace Jesus Christ as the only Mediator of rescue and revelation (1 Corinthians 8:4-6).

Foundations

Day 7: Spiritual experiences can't replace Jesus

FRAMEWORKS

Modern people might reject religion out of a desire for rationalism, but there are others that reject institutional religion for a kind of "New Age spirituality".

The 19th century was divided between rationalism and romanticism: whereas some felt that the path to knowledge lay through reason and science, there were plenty of others who rebelled against a rationalist reductionism and explored a romanticism of experience, mysticism, art, music and poetry.

The same impetus is as strong as ever. It is a very old tradition but has a new energy with postmodern people who have an almost allergic reaction against authority and structures.

The mystics with their spiritual ecstasies have often looked down on the philosophers with their logic. However, though the Bible agrees that the human mind is darkened through evil behaviour, the human spirit is no better.

Paul wrote a letter to a new Church family at the heart of the ancient city of Ephesus. This city was the centre for the worship of the goddess Artemis, the goddess of the hunt, wildness and the Moon. Her temple was considered to be one of the wonders of the ancient world. Acts 19:35 seems to indicate that a strange meteor was at the heart of that incredible temple – and it was said that those who were allowed into the innermost shrine had a powerful spiritual experience of encounter with the goddess. It sounds like a place of profound spirituality and yet Paul wrote two of the most disturbing verses in the Bible.

Ephesians 2:1-2 – "As for you, you were dead in your transgressions and sins, in which you used to live when you followed the ways of this world and of the ruler of the kingdom of the air, the spirit who is now at work in those who are disobedient.

Yes, the ancient Ephesians were very spiritual people and they were very in touch with the spiritual world, following a goddess of wild moonlit nights and the thrill of the hunt.

SEEING BEYOND RELIGION?

For those who can't handle the structure and authority of classic religions, the appeal of a non-specific spirituality is very appealing.

Instead of submitting to the religious traditions, some prefer to make their own private choices – taking a bit of Buddhism, yoga, a sprinkling of seasonal Christianity and possibly a portion of old paganism.

The idea is that true spirituality is beyond and above all the religious traditions. If we are all innately divine or innately capable of connecting to the divine, then choices that feel right to us individually need no further justification.

The problem is that claiming to have a superior insight, above all the world's religions is quite a claim!

A person might say something like, "well, of course, all these religions are local versions of my god, my ultimate spiritual reality. They are all attempts to conceive my god or aspects of my ultimate reality. All the world's religions are groping in the dark after the reality that I have discovered, that I experience. **They** don't realise it, but they are all dealing with **my** god."

A famous exponent of this kind of thinking put it like this. Imagine some blind-folded people bumping into an elephant. One grabs its trunk and says, "This is some kind of snake". Another hugs its leg and says "No, it seems to be a kind of tree".
Another rubs its huge side and declares, "It is more like a large rock".

Of course, says the observer, they are all mistaken because I can see that it is in fact an elephant.

It's a clever little parable, but the observer believes that they have no blindfold on. They think that they can see reality as it is. They tend to imagine that the world's religions are secretly tapping into the ultimate truth that they have so easily connected to.

This view perhaps seemed to be inclusive at first, but when we look at it more carefully it is totally exclusive. In the end my super-god or ultimate reality is the real one – and all the others are mistaken

In contrast to all this, Bernard of Clairvaux in his 12th sermon on the Song of Songs gives us a Christ-centred, Church-centred mysticism:

"although none of us will dare arrogate for his own soul the title of bride of the Lord, nevertheless we are members of the Church which rightly boasts of this title and of the reality which it signifies, and hence may justifiably assume a share in her honor. For what all of us simultaneously possess in a full and perfect manner, that each one of us undoubtedly possesses by participation.

Thank you, Lord Jesus, for your kindness in uniting us to the Church you so dearly love, not merely that we may be endowed with the gift of faith, but that like brides we may be one with you in an embrace that is sweet, chaste, and eternal, beholding with unveiled faces that glory which is yours in union with the Father and the Holy Spirit for ever and ever. Amen."

Yet, the Word of God says that their spiritual life was really a kind of spiritual death and that the spirit of the air was at work in them [the devil].

In a culture that has been materialistic for many generations, many people find a certain liberation in discovering "spirituality".

However, there are many spirits out there, and they are not good for us. They may offer to be our guide, give us dreams, visions, and even miraculous powers [as in Acts 16:16] – but none of them can guide us into the life of the Eternal God.

New Age mysticism includes the idea that by opening up our minds and spirits to spiritual realities, we can connect to the divine light and life. However, Jesus was in constant **confrontation** with spiritual forces throughout the gospels.

Modern spirituality has a very naïve view of the human spirit. Jeremiah 17:9 tells us that far from finding the divine within ourselves we find an incomprehensible heart of deceit and wickedness – a heart that we cannot master or fathom.

Only the LORD God can handle the darkness of the human heart.

> Examine Ephesians 2:3-6.
> What was our spiritual position before we were rescued by Jesus?
> What was the possible range of spiritual experience available to us?
> Was it possible to reach beyond that without Jesus? What did it take to open up positive religious experiences for us?

There IS a route into the heights of spiritual life and experience, but it is not through general "spirituality" or new age mysticism. Jesus Christ alone can lift us from the death of our wickedness to the heights of heaven so that we can sit with Him in the glory of the Father and the Spirit.

Christian mystics have an intense concentration on Jesus and through Him experience the life of God in extraordinary ways: for example, Macrina of Cappadocia, Bernard of Clairvaux and Thomas a Kempis.

Foundations

Day 8: Jesus really is the Living God

FRAMEWORKS

When modern people begin to think about coming to know the Eternal Living God we often assume that it is possible to begin with a general or partial knowledge of God which can build up into a fuller knowledge of God.

In one sense that is obviously true because we will always be going ever deeper into the knowledge of the Infinite God – but at another level it can be seriously mistaken.

Earlier we noted how modern people sometimes assume that there has been an evolution of religion from animism, through polytheism, onto monotheism and then possibly onto Trinitarianism.

However, in the Bible from the very earliest times, from 2000 BC, the ancient church was fully Trinitarian. Moses, in the book of Genesis, might not use the language that became common after the Nicene Creed, but he clearly takes it for granted that there is an Unseen LORD, the Angel of the LORD and the Spirit of the LORD who are together the one LORD God.

In other words, the most ancient church is clearly encountering the exact same Trinitarian God that we do today. There is no sense that the Living God was appearing to them or revealing Himself to them in a different way or a partial way. Jesus Christ is the same yesterday, today and forever [Hebrews 13:8].

This is profoundly significant because it goes to the very heart of salvation and revelation.

> Read Deuteronomy 32:1-43. It is the long song of Moses right at the end of his life. Count up the times that Moses refers to the LORD God as the "Rock".
>
> Now, read 1 Corinthians 10:1-4. Who was the Rock that Moses spoke about?

COMPLETELY REVEALED AND COMPLETELY HIDDEN!

When Jesus encounters us He not only reveals the Living God just as He is – in all His Trinitarian wonder and glory, but He also shows that all our human ideas about God are completely wrong. When we think about the LORD God we only have these human words and concepts that are full of false assumptions, pride, pagan baggage and confusion. Nevertheless, when Jesus encounters us He takes hold of us and makes the Infinite and Living God known, even using all our flimsy words and confused ideas!

The "God" that we have in our sinful human minds cannot be seen, because in the end it is an illusion or a delusion. Yet, the real and Living God shows up to openly and honestly show Himself as He really is – always causing our assumptions and pride to be smashed down!

"We must actually say (that the Living God in Jesus is) wholly revealed and wholly concealed at one and the same time. We must say wholly revealed because by the grace of revelation our human views and concepts are invited and exalted to share in the truth of God and therefore in a marvellous way made instruments of a real knowledge of God (in His being for us and as He is in Himself).

We must say wholly concealed because our human views and concepts (the only ones at our disposal for the knowledge of God, and claimed by God Himself as a means to this end) have not in themselves the smallest capacity to apprehend God…

In both ways, through His self-disclosure and His concealment, He is at one and the same time knowable and unknowable to us. In other words, in His self-revelation and concealment He has become for us an object of our human knowledge while remaining completely unknowable to us…

We have thus to recognise Him both in His hiddenness and in His self-disclosure. It will certainly be true that in both cases He remains completely unknowable to us even as we may and must know Him.
In all our thinking and speaking about Him we never become His masters.

We are always and must always be His servants, and indeed quite unprofitable servants. But it is also true—and this must be stated just as vigorously—that in both cases He becomes completely recognisable by us, not because of our capacity, thinking and speaking, but because of the grace of His revelation… God has revealed Himself in Jesus Christ." (Karl Barth, *Church Dogmatics*, Volume 1, part 2, section 29).

The LORD God appeared to people just as He really is – right from the beginning of the world.

He doesn't seem to appear as a non-Trinitarian God at any time! He is always revealed through the Eternal Son in the power of the Spirit.

Does the Living God play games with us?
One person asked this: did God play peek-a-boo with His ancient people, never really allowing them to see Him as He really is? Did He hide the most important aspects of Himself because…. Well, why? Why would the Living God treat His ancient church in a different way? Were they not smart enough?

Did they need to get used to a kind of unitarian monotheism first before moving onto the Trinity?

Did the LORD God deliberately give the impression that He was one thing before showing Himself to be something else later? Was it orthodox to be unitarian in the Old Testament but not in the New Testament?
Could you be saved without knowing God the Son in the Old Testament but not in the New Testament?

Often modern people assume that ancient people were stupid, unthinking and much less civilised than us. However, the Bible doesn't see people in that way and if we are honest about the modern world, it is not especially smart or civilised.

The idea that ancient people had simpler views of theology or religion is false. If you read a book called "Against Heresies" by bishop Irenaeus of the 2nd century he outlines Gnostic religious ideas that are bewilderingly complicated. These Gnostic religions can be traced back to much older times in Persia. The religions of ancient Babylon or Egypt are also complex and sophisticated.

If the **pagan** people could handle complex religions, why would the Living God treat His own holy people as if they were uniquely stupid?

The Living God does not play games. He encounters His people just as He is. We cannot comprehensively understand everything about Him, but we can truly know Him. From Genesis to Revelation the Father sends His Son in the power of the Spirit to create, reveal and redeem.

Foundations

Day 9: What IS a partial knowledge of God?

FRAMEWORKS

We have considered the possibility that the Living God deliberately made partial or misleading revelations of Himself. He encounters His people as He is – or else He does not encounter us at all!

However, even if He does fully reveal Himself as He is, with no "lisping in His speech" or disguises in His appearance, even the holiest of His saints cannot grasp all that He is!

Our knowledge of God through Jesus is true but not exhaustive.

Now, theologians and philosophers sometimes talk about people having a partial knowledge of God.

What is the difference between a partial knowledge of God and a false knowledge of God? That is a serious question for us to consider.

If I believed that God was like a large apple or that God is confined to the planet Mercury, would we describe those ideas as a partial knowledge of God or completely false ideas of God? If the Bible and Church teaching are our guides, then we must say that such statements are entirely false.

Now, what if I said that there is one God, but that God is a single person. To a person who loves Jesus and worships the trinity, isn't that statement just as bizarre and outrageous, even blasphemous, as the other ones about being like an apple or being confined on Mercury?

If somebody said that the most basic essence of their God is infinite power and timelessness, wouldn't we assume they knew nothing of Jesus Christ? Pagan philosophy starts from very different foundations than Church. One great Church theologian said that whatever god is "proved" by philosophy cannot be the Living God of the Bible.

Theism leads to atheism

Jurgen Moltmann's book *The Crucified God* tackles the "theism" that had replaced the Living God in much of Western Christianity.

Theism was created out of human ideas about power and politics, and gave rise to false religion. Atheism is the rejection of **that** God—and rightly so. Only Jesus is the answer to both theism and atheism.

"In the great period of the origin of theistic philosophy and theology, which essentially led to Islam, thought took three main lines:

1. God in the image of the imperial ruler;

2. God in the image of the personification of moral energy;

3. God in the image of the final principle of philosophy.

But measured by the origin of Christian faith in the crucified Christ, these three images are idols. This theism is tantamount to idolatry....

It follows, conversely, that theism removes man from his humanity and alienates him from his freedom, his joy and his true being. 'If man is free, then there is no such God; if there is such a God, then man is not free.' These are the alternatives in the face of such an idol.

A God who is conceived of in his omnipotence, perfection and infinity at man's expense cannot be the God who is love in the cross of Jesus, who makes a human encounter in order to restore their lost humanity to unhappy and proud divinities, who 'became poor to make many rich'.

God conceived of at man's expense cannot be the Father of Jesus Christ.

Zinzendorf saw this rightly when he complained of the 'legalistic and servile situation of the human race in face of God'.

'So-called Christianity has preserved the princely idea of God and blotted out the idea of the lamb, his merit and his death.'

It is indispensable for the liberated believer to dispense with the inhuman God, a God without Jesus, for the sake of the cross...

With a trinitarian theology of the cross faith escapes the dispute between and the alternative of theism and atheism: God is not only other-worldly but also this-worldly; he is not only God, but also man; he is not only rule, authority and law but the event of suffering, liberating love."
(Moltmann, *The Crucified God*, chapter 6, section 6).

When our Church ancestors formulated the Nicene Creed they wanted to get to the true essence of the Living God – and so they confessed the Father, Son and Holy Spirit, with especial concern to lift up and display Jesus Christ.

Whenever we want to speak about the very essence or nature of the Living God we will start to speak about Jesus who is sent by the Father in the power of the Spirit. We can't say anything about God without talking about Jesus!

So, even a partial knowledge of God must include **something** about Jesus, the Eternal Son of the Father, the Angel of the LORD, the Word of the Father. Descriptions of a god that do not mention Jesus or the Father or the Holy Spirit must be descriptions of some other god, some other philosophical idea.

> Take a blank sheet and just brainstorm all that we can actually know about the Living God through Jesus. Just make quick bullet points about Jesus, the Father and the Spirit. What have they done? What kind of life does this One God lead? How does the God of the Bible create, reveal, rescue and speak? What pleases the LORD God and what angers Him?
>
> Try to write down a simple definition of the nature of this God, the divine nature? Please complete this task before going any further.

Think about all that we can know about God and the deepest nature of the Living God. The truth is that the Living God speaks all this truth with simple honesty in the creation, in history, even in our very souls and bodies.

When a father or mother cares for their child, the nature of the Living God is being preached; when an animal dies to give food to another, the Cross is presented; when we see the sun rising to defeat the darkness we see the triumph of Jesus day after day.

We will come back to this truth soon, but for now read Romans 1:18-25 and see how as far as the Living God is concerned the whole of humanity has no excuse: what may be known about God is plain to everybody, even that mysterious Trinitarian nature and even His invisible qualities! Yes, He has made even His invisible qualities obvious to everybody!

Foundations

Day 10: Jesus must be our starting point

FRAMEWORKS

Bishop Lesslie Newbiggin had been a missionary bishop in South India for many years. When he came back to the UK in his retirement, he had a new lease of life as a theologian who called us back to those core truths of Jesus, the Trinity and the Bible.

He used to paraphrase what the ancient African theologian Athanasius said in Discourse 4, sections 6-7:

The only system of thought into which Jesus Christ will fit, is the one in which He is the starting point.

This means that if we are going to take Jesus seriously... if we are going to understand who Jesus really is and why the whole history of the universe moves around Him... we have to change **everything** that we think. We cannot simply adjust the systems of thought we already have and try to fit Him in. No! We have to basically start from scratch and build everything around Him.

Whenever people have really done **that** amazing things have happened. When people take Jesus as their starting point, civilisations emerge, cathedrals rise, universities are founded, the modern scientific project happens, operas are written, symphonies are composed, bridges are built, hospitals are founded and anything is possible.

> Read Isaiah 40:1-31, slowly and thoughtfully. Notice the prophecy of John the Baptist in verse 3 – Matthew 3:3. Then see how the LORD that John was preparing for did actually come – verses 9-11. Now absorb the enormity of this LORD Jesus in relation to time and space throughout the chapter, but how He uses that vast power in the final verses.
>
> How could this Jesus fit into any human system?

Whenever we try to contain Jesus Christ within one of our systems of thought we end up with a fake Jesus.

ATHANASIUS AND THE ARIANS

We have been back to Athanasius and the Arians several times in our studies so far.

The reason for this is that the fourth century was one of those moments in history when local churches, all over the world, took a very serious stand for Jesus as the starting point, the foundation, the centre, the beginning and the end.

Arius was that heretic who held onto all his old Greek philosophy and then tried to make Jesus fit into that system. He was probably sure that he had got a good grip on truth and reality. He had perhaps been so impressed with the insights and reasoning of the great experts of his day that he was not prepared to change those Greek philosophical foundations. Jesus had to somehow fit into that system.

The same thing has happened at other times. In parts of medieval Europe many people felt sure that Aristotle had come up with the perfect system of thought – and so some of them tried to describe Jesus using Aristotle's framework.

It might sound very strange. Why would people try to fit the Infinite God, the LORD Jesus into the speculations of some ancient Greek? Yet, that is what happened. Aristotle's system just seemed so brilliant, so final, so complete. Surely Jesus can fit into such a brilliant system!

In our own day we might laugh at these ancient people getting so fixed on the systems of their day... BUT, don't we do it as well?

Don't **we** try to fit Jesus into what we believe about the world, or psychology or sexuality or science?

Do we really make Jesus the starting point and test everything else by Him?

What is the test of truth in our own minds? How do we **know** what is true?

Is Jesus really our standard of truth – or do we make Him submit to other standards of truth that we hold **higher** than Him?

J. M. Neale's version of Prudentius' hymn from the 4th century:

Of the Father's love begotten
ere the worlds began to be,
He is Alpha and Omega,
He the Source, the Ending He,
of the things that are, that have been,
and that future years shall see,
evermore and evermore!

This is He whom heav'n-taught singers
sang of old with one accord,
whom the Scriptures of the prophets
promised in their faithful word;
now He shines, the long-expected;
let creation praise its Lord,
evermore and evermore!

Christ, to thee, with God the Father,
and, O Holy Ghost, to thee,
hymn and chant and high thanksgiving
and unwearied praises be,
honour, glory, and dominion
and eternal victory,
evermore and evermore!

We have seen that when ancient Christians tried to fit Jesus within the systems of Greek philosophy which were hostile to physical life, they couldn't cope with the full divinity of Jesus.

When others tried to fit Jesus into Roman systems of law, which believed in the idea of blind justice, they ended up seeing the Cross of Jesus as a harsh, commercial transaction. In the Bible justice starts from compassion and rescue, but only ends with vengeance, whereas the Roman system of justice begins and ends with vengeance.

When people have tried to fit Jesus into Hindu religious systems, He ends up being another avatar alongside other similar divine figures. His uniqueness is lost.

Some have tried to reduce the divine titles of Jesus to forms that would be acceptable to mainstream Islam, but in the process they lose Jesus as the fullness of God, the true bearer of the name of God. In finding a Jesus that fits in the Islamic system, they lose the God of the Bible.

In modern Europe and America, a reductionist view of science has led to a strongly materialistic view of truth. For 200 years many have tried to fit Jesus into that system of thought, but they have only ever ended up with a great human being – perhaps with the highest God-consciousness there has ever been; perhaps with the best teaching for humanity... but in the end, not divine but purely human.

In more recent years, the dominant religious system for much of the Western world has been called moralistic, therapeutic deism – some morals to do with the environment and social justice, the idea that spirituality is supposed to make us feel better about ourselves but with a god who stays out of our business. Attempts to fit Jesus into this system have obviously failed.

The point is clear: we are always going to be faced with systems of thought that seem obviously true, impossible to question – as every age has done. Yet, when we try to fit the LORD Jesus Christ into any system of thought we will lose the full reality of Jesus. We will be left with a husk and shadow.

Jesus Christ is the Alpha and the Omega; the beginning and the end – of all things. It is on this truth that we make our stand. It is the foundation on which we build the only system into which He will fit.

Foundations

Day 11: Jesus is not just part of the picture

FRAMEWORKS

Jesus is not part of a bigger picture.

This is one of the vital blocks in the foundation of Church life and thought. It is at the heart of the whole Bible from start to finish.

Jesus is not an introduction to theology.
He is not simply the doorman into some bigger reality.
He is not a piece in a jigsaw.

He is the big picture.

If Jesus is the starting point, as we saw in our last study, then He is also the finishing point. We never move on beyond Jesus to something bigger. He is the very biggest reality that there is: in Him all the fullness of the Deity lives in bodily form [Colossians 2:9].

Paul's wrote to the church at Colossae because they thought that Jesus was simply part of a bigger picture.

The Colossian church trusted in Jesus and were obviously excited about Him, but they had already got lots of things in their picture of reality.

In Colossians 2:16-19 Paul tells them not to think of diet, time, angels or self-improvement as realities to placed alongside Jesus Himself.

"do not let anyone judge you by what you eat or drink, or with regard to a religious festival, a New Moon celebration or a Sabbath day. These are a shadow of the things that were to come. The reality, however, is found in Christ.

Do not let anyone who delights in false humility and the worship of angels disqualify you. Such a person also goes into great detail about what they have seen; they are puffed up with idle notions by their unspiritual mind. They have lost connection with the head, from whom the whole body, supported and held together by its ligaments and sinews, grows as God causes it to grow."

JESUS ABOVE ALL OTHERS

In W Dillistone's book on "The Christian Understanding of Atonement" he quotes Arnold Toynbee's remarkable conclusion to his study of history.

Is there any evidence in his great study of history for a pattern to make sense of it all? Is there any suggestion of that which would give meaning to the whole of history?

"This is the final result of our survey of saviours.

When we first set out on our quest we found ourselves in the midst of a mighty marching host; but as we have pressed forward on our way, the marchers company by company have been falling out of the race.

The first to fall were the swordsmen, the next the archaists, the next the futurists, the next the philosophers, until at length there were no more human competitors left in the running.

In the last stage of all our motley host of would-be saviours, human and divine, has dwindled to a single company of none but gods; and now the strain has been testing the staying power of these last remaining runners, notwithstanding their superhuman strength.

At the final ordeal of death few even of these would-be saviour-gods have dared to put their title to the test by plunging into the icy river.

And now, as we stand and gaze with our eyes fixed upon the farther shore, a single figure rises from the flood and straightway fills the whole horizon.

There is the Saviour; "and the pleasure of the LORD shall prosper in his hand: he shall see of the travail of his soul and shall be satisfied."

Spurgeon preaching on Colossians 1:19 –

"It pleased the Father that *in Him* should all fulness dwell."

Where else could all fulness have been placed? There was wanted a vast *capacity to contain* "all fulness." Where dwells there a being with nature capacious enough to compass within himself all fulness?

As well might we ask, "Who hath measured the waters in the hollow of His hand, and meted out heaven with the span, and comprehended the dust of the earth in a measure, and weighed the mountains in scales, and the hills in a balance?"

To Him only could it belong to contain "all fulness," for He must be equal with God, the Infinite. How suitable was the Son of the Highest, who "was by Him, as one brought up with Him," to become the grand storehouse of all the treasures of wisdom, and knowledge, and grace, and salvation.

Moreover, there was wanted not only capacity to contain, but *immutability to retain* the fulness, for the text says, "It pleased the Father that in Him should all fulness *dwell*," that is, abide, and remain, for ever.

Now if any kind of fulness could be put into us mutable creatures, yet by reason of our frailty we should prove but broken cisterns that can hold no water.

The Redeemer is Jesus Christ, the same yesterday, to-day, and forever: therefore, was it meet that all fulness should be placed in Him. "The Son abideth ever." "He is a priest for ever after the order of Melchisedec." "Being made perfect he became the author of eternal salvation unto all them that obey him." "His name shall endure forever: His name shall be continued as long as the sun: and men shall be blessed in Him: all nations shall call Him blessed."

There must have been many things that seemed vital parts of reality: the ancient Law of Moses, diet or fasting plans, insights into angels, psychological therapy, powerful rituals, traditional festivals and physical exercise programmes.

There may well be reflections of reality in some or all of these things, but they are only shadows, fragments of the full reality which is found in Jesus Christ alone.

> Read Colossians 1:15-20. Take time to chew on the comprehensive nature of Jesus – how He includes everything else within Him.
>
> Jesus is the context for everything in the heavens and on earth. There is nothing bigger or beyond Him.

In our own time, there are all kinds of powerful systems of thought and traditions; all kinds of experiences; all kinds of therapies and treatments; all kinds of ideas about health and fitness.

None of these are the key to reality.

None of them are the substance of reality; the centre that holds every part in place.

None of these things explain everything else.

The LORD Jesus Christ created everything, with the plans of His Father and the power of the Spirit.

He alone is the Head over **EVERYTHING**.

If we treat Him as merely a **part** of the picture, we become disconnected from Him and then will lose life itself.

Foundations

Day 12: Jesus created the universe

FRAMEWORKS

Everything in the heavens and on the earth was created by Jesus Christ.

We have said this several times so far, but now we need to take time to mediate on this foundational truth.

Many people, even people who call themselves Christians, see Jesus as simply a person who popped up in the middle of history. I have even heard sermons that speak as if the Old Testament was just "God" and then Jesus came along to save people only in the New Testament!

That is NOT how the Bible and Church sees Jesus!

> Read John 1:1-10 and then read Genesis 1:1-5.
>
> Let's imagine that John had Genesis chapter 1 on his desk a he was beginning to write his biography of Jesus. He wanted us to see what Moses was talking about. He is almost writing a commentary on those first verses of Genesis. What does John want us to see in that original text? Who was God speaking to in Genesis 1? Why did the Eternal God need to speak at all? What was the source of light on that first day?
>
> Take time to meditate on these questions and Genesis 1. There are many treasures waiting in that first chapter of the Bible!

Jesus is the Eternal Son of the Father. We will think a lot more deeply about what that means in the Module on God, but for now it is important to realise that Jesus was the Son of the Father and the Spirit eternal ages before the universe began.

There never was a time when He did not exist – and before He was born of the Virgin Mary He didn't spend endless years sitting on His hands wondering what to do.

The Father initiated the work of Creation: He willed and planned it all. However, Jesus was the Craftsman, the Builder, who put it all together.

THE WITNESS OF EARLIER AGES

Cyril of Jerusalem [313-386 AD] in his lectures to train up new converts [12:24] said:

"Christ is the Only-begotten Son of God and Maker of the World, for "He was in the world, and the world was made through Him, and "He came unto His own," as the Gospel teaches us.

But Christ is the Maker, at the bidding of the Father, not only of things visible but also things invisible.

For, according to the apostle: "In Him were created all things in the heavens or on the earth, things visible and things invisible, whether thrones, or dominations, or principalities, or powers. All things have been created through Him and unto Him, and He is before all creatures, and in Him all things hold together."

Even if you talked about other worlds, Jesus Christ, at the bidding of the Father, is Maker of these too."

When Augustine quoted Jesus in John 8:58 he said:

"Before Abraham I am"; that's what Jesus said Himself, the Gospel speaks. Listen to it or read it. Being the creator before Abraham; he's the creator before Adam, creator before heaven and earth, before all the angels, and the whole spiritual creation, "thrones, dominions, principalities and powers," creator before all things whatsoever."

There was a wonderful theologian called Hilary of Poitiers who lived from 315-367 AD. His great obsession was to lift up Jesus as truly and completely Divine, just as much as the Father and the Spirit. He thought about Jesus as Creator and concluded:

"There is no doubt that all things are through the Son, since, according to the apostle, "All things are through Him and in Him."

If all things are through Him, and all things are from nothing, and nothing exists except through Him, I ask in what way does He lack the true nature of God, since he is not lacking either in the nature or the power of God?

For He used the power of His nature that these things should exist which had no existence, and that these things should exist which pleased Him."

Hilary could see that if Jesus had the power and authority to create everything that has ever come into existence, then that seems to be strong proof that He is God at full strength.

God spoke His Word – and that Word actually made everything happen.

We have looked at Colossians 1 before but notice again verses 15-16 – "The Son is the image of the invisible God, the firstborn over all creation. For in Him all things were created: things in heaven and on earth, visible and invisible, whether thrones or powers or rulers or authorities; all things have been created through Him and for Him."

What is a "firstborn" in the Bible? It is the one who inherits everything. Jesus created everything and He is the true inheritor of everything in the universe.

Proverbs chapter 8 has provoked great debate since the 4th century because it describes Wisdom, who was there at the creation of all things always being born from the Father. Some have rightly said that Wisdom could be the Holy Spirit, but in the 4th century they all thought it was Jesus, the Eternal Son. Some thought it showed that Jesus was born when the universe began, but the Church's view, enshrined in the Nicene Creed, is that Jesus is always born from His Father, always affirmed and confirmed as His Eternal Son.

However, listen to these verses describing the Divine Craftsman who was with the Father in the creation of the world. Here from the New American Standard Bible.

"While He had not yet made the earth and the fields, Nor the first dust of the world, when He established the heavens, I was there. When He inscribed a circle on the face of the deep, when He made firm the skies above, when the springs of the deep became fixed, when He set for the sea its boundary so that the water would not transgress His command, when He marked out the foundations of the earth; then I was beside Him, a Master Workman; And I was daily [His] delight, rejoicing always before Him, rejoicing in the world, His earth, And [having] my delight in the sons of men.."

Jesus is not just the foundation for our theology; He is the foundation for the universe itself.

Foundations

Day 13: Jesus holds the universe together

FRAMEWORKS

Do "the laws of nature" hold the universe together?

For many modern people the universal explanation for everything in the universe are "the laws of nature": but even if there really are such "laws", who wrote them? Laws need to be written and enforced.

Are we to imagine that the basic elements of the universe are **self**-organising and **self**-governing? Do the atoms just "know" how to organise together? Why do they so reliably behave in the same way? Some people might be happy to say "well, that's just the way it is", but that kind of answer has not satisfied most people down the ages, all over the world.

Mathematics is a very philosophically complex subject. Do numbers "exist"? Can we see a number 7 or weigh the number 153? Numbers seem to be something that only exist in human minds. Yet, the universe clearly runs mathematically. There are specific mathematical formula that describe all kinds of features of the world around us. How can this be?

In both the book of Genesis and at the beginning of John's gospel, Jesus is introduced as The Word – the Logos. He is the very logic of the universe. He is the reason that there is unity underlying such glorious diversity and complexity. He has been described as the operating system of the universe.

The first Christmas was the moment when the very life, soul, light and logic of the universe became a human being.

Think about how He did His miracles and how He interacted with the world around Him. He didn't even need to **pray** to make anything happen – as all the prophets and apostles do. No! Jesus just told the world what to do – or even just did impossible things without even asking or telling!

CREATION AND CHRIST

Colossians 1:16 & 17, together with John 1 and Hebrews 1, show us that the Son is the matrix or the blueprint of the creation – its character and destiny conformed to Him.

He is the Logos, the scheme, by which the creation holds together – and this is as true for the visible as for the invisible creation. The seen creation is no less suitable for God than the unseen.

In fact, as we will see, the purposes of God find their resting place in the seen creation, not in the unseen. All this teaches us that the universe is not at odds with God in any way.

Sometimes people talk as if the big thing that divides us from God is that He is the Creator and we are the creatures. This isn't the problem at all. This has only become any issue because we are **sinners** and He is **holy**.

The creation is not against God: it reveals God – it declares the glory of God, it preaches Christ day and night.

God does not have to adapt Himself to some kind of alien environment when He engages with the universe.

The heavens and the earth are what He created, and it has all been designed by Him as a place where He can be known, where He can be Himself.

This is why the Incarnation is not an illogical or incomprehensible absurdity – it is nothing but a natural complement of the Biblical doctrine of creation.

In Lightfoot's classic commentary on Colossians, speaking of 1:16, he says:

"THE heresy of the Colossian teachers took its rise ... in their cosmical speculations. It was therefore natural that the Apostle in replying should lay stress on the function of the Word in the creation and government of the world.

This is the aspect of His work most prominent in the first of the two distinctly Christological passages.

The Apostle there predicates of the Word [the Son] not only prior but absolute existence.

All things were created by Him, are sustained in Him, are tending towards Him.

Thus He is the beginning, middle, and end of creation.

This He is because He is the very *Image* of the Invisible God, because in Him dwells the Plenitude of Deity.

This creative and administrative work of Christ the Word [the Son] in the natural order of things is always emphasized in the writings of the Apostles when they touch on the doctrine of His Person ...

With ourselves this idea has retired very much into the background ... And the loss is serious."

He walked on water; produced infinite food from one packed lunch; turned water into wine; raised the dead; controlled the weather; knew what people were thinking; and cured every disease.

Jesus could modify the operating instructions of the universe as and when He wanted!

Defining a "miracle" has been hotly debated down the ages. In modern times it is often called "an event that breaks the laws of nature". However, if Jesus essentially IS the "law of nature", then He never needs to break the laws or "break into" His own universe!

The "laws of nature" are how Jesus normally runs the universe, but very occasionally He does things differently.

We should learn to see everything that happens as a "miracle" of divine work. In the Bible the tides, the weather, the sunrise, the way animals find their food, the way the trees grow and crops come to harvest... all of these are described as the glorious working of the LORD God.

None of these things just happen by their own power or their own "logic"!

These are deep things to think about!

> Read Hebrews 1:1-4.
>
> The ancient prophets spoke about Jesus for thousands of years – but most people never got to meet Him. Even the prophets received visions and dreams about Him. Yet, in the end Jesus pushed aside all the prophets and spoke for Himself!
>
> Describe Jesus using just these verses from the beginning of Hebrews. What is His relationship to the universe?

Foundations

Day 14: Jesus is the original model for humanity

FRAMEWORKS

Jesus is the original, eternal pattern from which human beings are copied.

He is the eternal Image of God, according to Colossians 1:15- and yet human beings are made "in the image of God", according to Genesis 1:26. He is the **eternal** image and humans are created copies.

If this is so, then He must be the foundation for all human life and thought.

Philo was one of the greatest Bible scholars of the ancient world, before the birth of Jesus. He was born in Alexandria in c. 35 BC and lived to perhaps 50 AD. It is said that when Mark planted his church in Alexandria that Philo came along to that Church and eventually travelled to Rome to meet Peter.

Whatever the case, Philo understood the great depths in Moses' account of the creation of humanity. He returned to it many times.

Philo knew that mere human beings could not mediate the being of God the Father: created human beings could not make the invisible Father visible to the universe!

Yet, Philo recognised that there is the Divine Word who is beside His Father and He is the true Image of God. In this Word (Logos) everything in the Father is expressed.

The Word is the pattern for all created things. The Eternal Son of the Father is the perfect expression of the Father, so He is able to impress that upon created things.

PHILO QUOTATIONS

"God does not seem to have used any other animal existing in creation as His model in the formation of humanity; but to have been guided, as I have said before, by his own Word (Logos) alone..."
Philo – *On Creation* XLVIII

"The Shadow of God is His Word (Logos), which He used like an instrument when He was making the world.

This Shadow or Model is the pattern of other things.

As God is Himself the model of that Image which He has now called His shadow, so also that Image is the model of other things.

He showed this when at the beginning of the Law when He said, "And God made man according to the image of God."

As the Image was modelled on God, so humanity was modelled on the Image..."
Philo – *Allegorical Interpretations* III

Noting that human beings were created in the image of God as physical beings, Philo notes how there is a much greater Image of God that is not part of the physical, created universe.

"[The man of Genesis 2:7] was created as a physical being who could be perceived by physical senses, but he was made in the likeness of a Being who could not be perceived by the senses, but only be the mind or soul...

...This is the Word (Logos) of God, the first beginning of all things, the original pattern or the archetypal idea, the first measure of the universe."
Philo – *Questions and Answers on Genesis*, Volume I, part 4.

"Why is it that God speaks as if of some other god, saying that He made man after the Image of God?

Why doesn't He just say that He made humanity after His **own** image? (Genesis 9:6).

This was a very accurate and appropriate statement uttered by God because no mortal creature could have been made in the image of the supreme Father of the universe. Rather, humanity was created after the pattern of the second Divine one, who is the Word (Logos) of the Supreme Being.

It is right that the rational soul or life of humanity be modelled on the divine Word..."
Philo – *Questions and Answers on Genesis*, Volume II.

Just as a priest stands between the people and the LORD God, so God the Son, the Eternal LORD Jesus, stands between the Father and all creation.

However, He has this **special** relationship with human beings, who are also given His special title of being in the image of God. Uniquely, above all other creatures, human beings are modelled on God the Son.

Isaiah 44:13 speaks of the human form "in all its glory". Why is the human form so glorious? It is because it is modelled on Christ Himself.

Think about how the Eternal Son formed us from the clay and then breathed life into us. Then, even when we sinned, in Adam & Eve, He came walking in the Garden to meet with His beloved creatures. All through the Bible He comes to eat with His people, even wrestle with Jacob!

The apostle Paul declares all this when he is thinking about the resurrection in 1 Corinthians 15:47-49. Adam was from the earth, but Jesus is **from heaven**.

Read 1 Corinthians 15:47-49 carefully. Can you see why Paul calls Jesus a "heavenly Man"?

> Read Psalm 8. It is about humanity and our place in the universe.
>
> Now read Hebrews 2:5-9. What point is the writer to the Hebrews making there? Why is it so important to see Jesus when we read Psalm 8?

Foundations

Day 15: Jesus is the Image of God

FRAMEWORKS

In the last study we saw how Jesus is the Image of God. Now we need to dig a little deeper into that.

Colossians 1:15 has been a theme verse throughout this Foundations course!

"The Son is the image of the invisible God."

The Greek word for "image" is *eikon*, from which we get the English word "icon".

An icon is a visual representation. We use them all the time on our phones and computers. When we click on an icon it opens up a much larger activity or program for us. The icon is the gateway into the larger experience. The icon expresses the heart of what it represents, so that when we see it we understand immediately what it is for.

Jesus is more than a shortcut to something bigger, though! Someone said that He is more like a window that gives us the view into the deepest, highest, greatest and fullest of all that the Living God is. That's better! Yet, He is more than just a window. He is Himself the deepest, highest, greatest and fullest of all that the Living God is.

Jesus is the fullness of God in bodily form.

Seeing is important. Some of the greatest theologians have suggested that intellectual "seeing" is all that matters: understanding God is far more important than merely seeing God with physical eyes. That does sound very spiritual and noble, but perhaps it doesn't take our physical form and the physical world seriously enough.

It is not enough to merely physically see someone to understand them. We spend time with them and listen to them. We get to know their ways and character, not all of which is easy to physically see. However, physically seeing is a very important part of knowing somebody.

THE SEVENTH ECUMENICAL COUNCIL

In 787 AD church leaders from all over the world gathered together to consider whether it is right to paint pictures of Jesus – and the other characters in the Bible.

After the death of Muhammad in 632 AD, the Islamic armies had not only conquered right across north Africa into Spain and France, but had also invaded the Persian and Byzantine empires to take huge expanses of the Middle East.

Islam believes that all images of created things are idolatrous. Allah has a very different view of the creation than Jesus Christ. In fact, when Christians teach that God became flesh, this is the worst sin of all to a Muslim, the unforgiveable sin of shirk.

Some Christians at the time thought that the rise of Islam was a judgement from God because they had made images in their churches, so they tried to destroy the images in agreement with the Islamic challenge.

However, in 787 the last of the great ecumenical councils gathered at Nicaea to consider this question. They decided that they had to display pictures of Jesus and the Bible characters to publicly show their faith that God became flesh and lived among us as Jesus.

Here are the main conclusions of the council:

"Venerating icons, having them in churches and homes, is what the Church teaches. They are "open books to remind us of God." Those who lack the time or learning to study theology need only to enter a church to see the mysteries of the Christian religion unfolded before them."

"Icons are necessary and essential because they protect the full and proper doctrine of the Incarnation. While God cannot be represented in His eternal nature ("...no man has seen God", John 1:18), He can be depicted simply because He "became human and took flesh."

Of Him who took a material body, material images can be made. In so taking a material body, God proved that matter can be redeemed. He deified matter, making it spirit-bearing, and so if flesh can be a medium for the Spirit, so can wood or paint, although in a different fashion."

One of the greatest theologians of that age was called John of Damascus (675-749). He debated with Muslims in Jerusalem about the Christian Faith and wrote a brilliant book called An Exact Exposition of the Orthodox Faith.

I do not worship matter, but the Creator of matter, who for my sake became material and deigned to dwell in matter, who through matter brought about my salvation...
—St. John of Damascus

For those of us who are blind, there is still the strong desire to touch a person's face to get a sense of what they "look like".

Jesus gave that great promise in Matthew 5:8 – "Blessed are the pure in heart, for they will see God." The intellectuals and philosophers might be happy to spend eternity merely thinking about God, but for the rest of us, to gaze at the beauty of the Living God, matters a very great deal.

However, to see the Father is no more than seeing the Son: Jesus is all that the Father is. In John 14:8-10, Philip wanted to gaze at the Father, but Jesus explained that trying to see over the head of Jesus misses the point of who Jesus is: He is the image of God. Everything that is in the Father is in Jesus.

"Philip said, "Lord, show us the Father and that will be enough for us." Jesus answered: "Don't you know me, Philip, even after I have been among you such a long time? Anyone who has seen me has seen the Father. How can you say, 'Show us the Father'? Don't you believe that I am in the Father, and that the Father is in me?"

No one has ever seen the Father at any time, yet it seems that one day Jesus will grant such a sight to us. What will we see? We will see all that we have already seen in the face of Jesus Christ. If we want to see what the Living God is really like, in the deepest mysteries and Most Holy Place, then give your time and your life to making Jesus the very centre of your vision.

> Read Exodus 33:7-11. Who was Moses meeting face to face in the Tent of Meeting? Could it be the Father or the Spirit?
>
> Notice that a man called Joshua (which is the Hebrew form of the name Jesus) almost lived in that tent with the LORD!
>
> Now read Exodus 33:18-34:9. Moses asks to see the LORD. How does the LORD answer Moses? Does this contradict what we read in 33:11?
>
> Notice an amazing thing in 34:9. There are two Lord's in that one verse. Why doesn't Moses say "if I have found favour in your eyes then YOU go with us"? Moses wanted to see the Lord in all His glory, but now he is happy for someone else called the Lord to travel with them. Why?

Foundations

Day 16: Jesus is the central character in the Bible

FRAMEWORKS

It's obvious that Jesus is the main character of the Gospels but think about His role in all the other books.

Luke begins the book of Acts by saying that in the Gospel he wrote about what Jesus **began** to do and teach until He ascended to heaven... with the implication that in this next volume he was going to look at what Jesus **continued to do** in and through His churches all over the world.

If that is true the book should not be called the Acts of the **Apostles** but the Acts of **Jesus**. The letters written to these churches in the rest of the New Testament are letters about these continuing **acts of Jesus**. The book of Revelation actually begins with Jesus writing His own letters to seven churches – and continues by showing that all the way through history, He is the main actor, the one on the throne.

But, what about the Old Testament?

The most basic Christian confession is "Jesus is Lord" (Romans 10:9; 1 Corinthians 12:3).

What does that mean? Often people think it means something like "Jesus is in charge; Jesus has authority", but it means far more than that. Even heretics like Jehovah's Witnesses can think that Jesus is in charge in some way.

When Paul uses the word "Lord" he is referring to that Old Testament name of the Living God: the LORD (Jehovah or Yahweh).

The key Christian confession is to recognise not just that Jesus is important or has authority, but that He is the LORD God of Israel, the One who was the central character from Genesis to Malachi.

He has always been sent from His Father in the power of the Spirit to be the Mediator in creation, revelation and redemption.

All the grace and truth in the Bible from beginning to end was always through Jesus, the Word (John 1:16-18).

IRENEAUS (130-202 AD)
AGAINST HERESIES
BOOK 4, CHAPTER 10

Chapter 10

The Old Testament Scriptures, and those written by Moses in particular, speak about the Son of God everywhere. They speak about His coming and passion ahead of time.

If this is true, then the Old Testament is obviously inspired by the same God as the New Testament.

In his gospel John records how the Lord spoke to the Jews: "You search the Scriptures and you think that you get eternal life from them. These are the Scriptures that speak about me, but you are not willing to come to Me to get life." (John 5:39-40).

How could those ancient Scriptures speak about Jesus unless they were from the very same God who was instructing people long before about the coming of His Son and telling them about the salvation brought by Him?

"If you had really believed Moses, then you would have also believed in Me, because Moses was writing about Me." (John 5:46).

Jesus said this, no doubt, because the Son of God is deeply rooted everywhere throughout the writings of Moses:

At one time the Son of God was speaking with Abraham just before He ate a meal with him.

At another time, He was giving the dimensions of the Ark to Noah.

He was the One who was looking for Adam in the Garden.

The Son of God also brought down judgement on the people of Sodom (Genesis 19).

He becomes **visible** (Genesis 12:7; 18:13; 31:11 etc etc).

He directs Jacob on his journey and spoke with Moses from the bush (Exodus 3:4).

It would be endless to recount the many times that Moses shows off the Son of God.

Of the passion and death of Jesus, Moses was not ignorant, but foretold it in a symbolic way in the Passover.

It was at that very feast of Passover our Lord suffered, though it had been proclaimed so long before.

Moses did not only describe the day but the place and the very time of day at which the sufferings ceased, together with the sign of the setting sun:

"You may not sacrifice the Passover within any other of your cities which the LORD God gives you, but only in the place which the LORD your God shall choose, where His Name shall be. You shall sacrifice the Passover at evening, when the sun sets." (Deuteronomy 16:5-6).

The Law as only a signpost pointing to Him – all the grace, forgiveness, cleansing and truth only ever came through Jesus. The Law itself cannot save anybody. Animal sacrifices do not make atonement for sin; water does not wash away guilt and shame.

The defining mark of the true saint is that they love Jesus Christ. We are to be joined to Him in a mystical marriage at the end of the world, at the marriage feast of the Lamb.

We obviously read the Gospels over and over again, because we love Him. We love to see Him at work and listen to His words. Yet, imagine that we found some more Gospels showing us more accounts of Jesus working and teaching! If we knew they were the true Word of God, wouldn't we be thrilled? Yet, once we start to read the Bible the way all our Christian ancestors read the Bible, we find that the whole Bible is full of Gospels – books showing off the words and works of Jesus Christ.

He has been speaking and acting since the world began, with just the same character and glory.

Have you ever wondered why so many modern people don't like the Old Testament – or struggle to read it or preach it? Have you noticed how often they have to have training sessions and conferences trying to persuade each other that there is a way to preach the Old Testament in a Christian way? They are trying to persuade themselves of something that they don't really feel or understand.

Once we recognise that Jesus is LORD then the Old Testament opens up like a treasure chest – and we can read it with the freedom and joy that the ancient and medieval churches were able to do.

> Can you think of examples of the LORD God acting in the Old Testament that seem to be Jesus? Look up Genesis 32:22-32 or Daniel chapter 3. Can you think of anymore?

The Old Testament is not about "God" in some vague and undefined sense. It has exactly the same Christian Faith as the New Testament: Trinitarian and Jesus-centred.

The Old Testament is about Church just as much as the New Testament. Acts 7:38 speaks of "the Church in the wilderness". It is Biblical to refer to the Old Testament people as Church.

NOTE: The Greek word for Church is "ecclesia". There is an Old Testament book that even has this word in its title!

Foundations

Day 17: Jesus has many titles

FRAMEWORKS

Getting to know the main glorious titles and names of the LORD Jesus Christ is a great help in reading the Bible.

If we are only looking for the name "Jesus" we will miss out on a great many times that He is speaking and acting! We will look at some of Moses' favourite ones in a couple of days, but for now we will get a big overview of some of the main ones, especially in the Old Testament.

> Take time to look up each of these titles of Jesus and read more of the context to get the full value from them. Old Testament quotations always contain even more treasure when you read the whole chapter they come from.

Redeemer

One of the oldest books in the Bible contains one of the dearest titles of the LORD Jesus. Job probably lived around 1800 BC, and when he was at one of the very lowest moments in those dark days, he suddenly had a clear vision of his only hope: Jesus, his Redeemer, who would stand on the earth and resurrect Job to see Him.
"As for me, I know that my Redeemer lives, and He will stand upon the earth at last." Job 19:25

Holy One of Israel

These tremendous words of encouragement were intended for the Church in exile, and so are heart-warming to the churches in every age. Repeating the title of Redeemer, here Isaiah shows us that the One who redeems us is utterly holy and pure.
"O Jacob don't be afraid, people of Israel, for I will help you. I am the LORD, your Redeemer. I am the Holy One of Israel." Isaiah 41:14

The Desire of All Nations & The LORD of Hosts

Jesus is the answer to every question. He fulfils the best desires of every nation in every age.

THE NAME OF JESUS

The great preacher C. H. Spurgeon preached many times on the name of Jesus.

On September 15th 1878 he began his sermon with these words:

"Bernard (of Clairvaux) has delightfully said that the name of Jesus is honey in the mouth, melody in the ear and joy in the heart. I rejoice in that expression on my own account, for it gives me my share of the delight and leads me to hope that while I am speaking, the sweetness of the precious name of Jesus may fill my own mouth.

Here also is a portion for you who are listening.

It is melody in the ear. If my voice should be harsh and my words discordant, you will yet have music of the choicest order, for the name itself is essential melody and my whole sermon will ring with its silver note.

May both speaker and hearer join in the third word of Bernard's sentence, and may we all find it to be joy in our hearts, a jubilee within our souls.

Jesus is the way to God, therefore will we preach Him. He is the truth, therefore will we hear of Him. He is the life, therefore shall our hearts rejoice in Him.

So inexpressibly fragrant is the name of Jesus that it imparts a delicious perfume to everything which comes in connection with it."

Preaching on Isaiah 9:6 in 1858, Spurgeon showed why Jesus has the name "Wonderful".

"if we can discern any brightness in our own hearts, or in the world's history, it can come from nowhere else, than from the one who is called "Wonderful, Counsellor, the mighty God."

The person spoken of in our text, is undoubtedly the Lord Jesus Christ. He is a child born, with reference to his human nature; he is born of the virgin, a child. But he is a son given, with reference to his divine nature, being given as well as born. Of course, the Godhead could not be born of woman. That was from everlasting, and is to everlasting. As a child he was born, as a son he was given.

"The government is upon his shoulder, and his name shall be called Wonderful."

Beloved, there are a thousand things in this world, that are called by names that do not belong to them; but in entering upon my text, I must announce at the very opening, that Christ is called Wonderful, because he is so. God the Father never gave his Son a name which he did not deserve...

As long as the moon endureth, there shall be found men, and angels, and glorified spirits, who shall always call him by his right name. "His name shall be called Wonderful.""

When people look for wisdom, truth, love, compassion, beauty, holiness, unity, forgiveness, healing, meaning or any other virtue, they find more than they dreamed in Jesus. He is the General over all the armies and powers of heaven: the LORD of Hosts, the Commander of the LORD's armies.
"I will shake all nations, and the Desire of all nations shall come: and I will fill this house with glory, saith the LORD of hosts." (King James Version of the Bible) Haggai 2:7.

Servant
One of the titles that means the most to Jesus Himself is the title of Servant. He did not come to be served, but to serve and give His life as a ransom for many. In that glorious description of his atoning death, Isaiah names Him, "Servant". **Isaiah 53:10-12**
"It was the LORD's will to crush Him and cause Him to suffer, and though the LORD makes His life an offering for sin, He will see His offspring and prolong His days, and the will of the LORD will prosper in His hand. After He has suffered, He will see the light of life and be satisfied; by His knowledge my Righteous Servant will justify many, and He will bear their iniquities."

Man of Sorrows or Suffering
From that same chapter, Isaiah gives Him a title that seems an insult, but when understood properly is a title of great honour.
"He was despised and rejected by mankind, a Man of Suffering, and familiar with pain. Like one from whom people hide their faces He was despised, and we held Him in low esteem." Isaiah 53:3

The LORD our righteousness
There are other titles given to Jesus in Jeremiah 23, but it is vital to know that He gives us His own righteousness.
"This is the name by which he will be called: The LORD Our Righteous Saviour." Jeremiah 23:6

Rose of Sharon.
The whole book of the Song of Songs is primarily about the love between Christ and His Church. On a secondary level there is helpful wisdom about marriage for us too, but how glorious are the titles of love for Jesus in this book!
"I am a rose of Sharon, a lily of the valleys." Song of Songs 2:1

Foundations

Day 18: Jesus taught that the Old Testament is about Him

FRAMEWORKS

In several of our studies we have seen Jesus in the Old Testament.

However, it has been suggested that this is just the interpretation of Christians who are trying to read meaning back into the Old Testament that was never intended by the original authors. Perhaps Church leaders go so carried away with the wonder of Jesus that they would force Him into all kinds of Biblical passages whether He was really there or not!

Jesus Himself taught this view of the Old Testament. He taught that He is the LORD God of Israel who met with Moses, Abraham and Isaiah.

NOTE: a few years ago there was a popular textbook that suggested that although Jesus taught the **truth** you could not follow His **methods** of Bible study because He was too influenced by the wrong methods of His time!

Let's begin with the amazing Bible studies that Jesus did after His resurrection. These church leaders were going all over the world planting churches, so they needed to show off Jesus from the Word of God. He showed them how to do it.

> Read Luke 24:13-53 and see how Jesus summarises the Old Testament first to the people on their way to Emmaus and then to the disciples.
>
> Try to express that summary in your own words and think of some Scriptures that Jesus may have shown them. Think about the texts that the apostles quoted themselves in the coming weeks and years.

Notice that He showed them Himself in "all the Scriptures" not just "some" Scriptures. A teacher some years ago said that he felt the Old Testament was like a few mountain tops on which you could see Christ clearly, but the rest was lower down valleys that were more obscure!

That's not how Jesus saw it!

THE SCRIPTURES SPEAK ABOUT JESUS

Irenaeus, commenting on John 5:45-47 says:

"Christ here indicates in the clearest possible way that the writings of Moses are His words. If, then, this is the case with Moses, then it is also beyond doubt that the words of the other prophets are His words as well." (*Against Heresies* – 4.2.3)

Matthew Henry, in his precious commentary on the whole Bible, opens up John 5:39-47:

"Note, It is possible for men to be very studious in the letter of the scripture, and yet to be strangers to the power and influence of it... Christ saith only, *You think* you have *eternal life* in the scriptures, because, though they did retain the belief and hope of eternal life, and grounded their expectations of it upon the scriptures, yet herein they missed it, that they looked for it by the bare reading and studying of the scripture. It was a common but corrupt saying among them, *He that has the words of the law has eternal life...*

[2.] We must *search the scriptures* **for Christ**, as the new and living *way* that leads to this *end*. These are *they*, the great and principal witnesses, *that testify of me*.

Note, *First*, The scriptures, even those of the Old Testament, *testify* of Christ, and by them God *bears witness* to Him.

The Spirit of Christ in the prophets testified beforehand of Him (1 Pt. 1:11), the purposes and promises of God concerning Him, and the previous notices of Him.

The Jews knew very well that the Old Testament testified of the Messiah, and were critical in their remarks upon the passages that looked that way; and yet were careless, and wretchedly overseen, in the application of them.

Secondly, Therefore we must *search the scriptures*, and may hope to find eternal life in that search, **because they testify of Christ**; for this is *life eternal, to know Him;* see 1 Jn. 5:11.

Christ is the treasure hid in the field of the scriptures, the water in those wells, the milk in those breasts...

Moses was a witness for Christ and to His doctrine (v. 46, 47): *He wrote of me.*

Moses did particularly prophesy of Christ, as the Seed of the woman, the Seed of Abraham, the Shiloh, the great Prophet; the ceremonies of the law of Moses were *figures of Him that was to come.*

The Jews made Moses the patron of their opposition to Christ; but Christ here shows them their error, that Moses was so far from writing against Christ that he wrote *for Him,* and *of Him.*"

It is worth looking quite carefully at Jesus' teaching in John 5:39-47. First Jesus acknowledges that they do study the Scriptures intensely, but they seemed to think that the Scriptures themselves were able to give life or save people. As much as we might love the Bible, the Bible cannot die for our sins, rise from the dead or ascend to the Father's throne!

As Jesus says, the only reason to study the Bible is to find Jesus and come to Him for life. Reading the Bible without seeing Jesus shows that the love of God is not in our hearts. Looking for glory from one another, from human scholarship or and approval excludes us from the glory of God.

Notice that it is Moses who will be the judge of those who study him without coming to Jesus – verse 45. Anyone who actually believes what Moses wrote would trust Jesus, before any of the New Testament had been written, before the Cross and Resurrection of Jesus.

Verse 47 is very deep and powerful. Jesus wonders how anybody will be able to believe in Him if they don't **already believe Moses**. In other words, Moses makes it easier to trust Jesus. Moses is easier to understand than Jesus – or Moses is God's inspired introduction to Jesus. Moses throws light onto Jesus.

Often in modern Bible studies it is said that Jesus throws light onto Moses and the Old Testament. One teacher even said that the Old Testament was darkness and mystery until Jesus came along and made sense of it! Jesus seemed to take the exact opposite view.

We might be tempted to give a person a copy of one of the gospels if they are enquiring about Jesus, but it might be more Biblical to give them a copy of Genesis or Exodus.

Foundations

Day 19: Moses really does speak about Jesus

FRAMEWORKS

Jesus insisted that Moses was talking about Him. Do we really believe that? Could Jesus have backed up such a claim?

In the first centuries of the Church after the apostles this view of the Old Testament was very common. For the first century or so many church leaders didn't have the New Testament at all and so they used only the Old Testament in preaching Jesus. It is well worth reading those wonderful ancient sisters and brothers who so carefully read Moses, the Prophets and the Writings (the ancient categories of the Scriptures).

Before we begin, notice how Moses renames his assistant from Oshea to Joshua (which is the name Jesus) - Numbers 13:16. The very first book after the books of Moses is simply called "Jesus".

Let's begin with the Angel of the LORD in this study.

> Read Genesis 16:1-16.
>
> Write down all you can about the Angel of the LORD?
>
> Could this be an angelic creature?

Verse 13 is important – "She gave this name to the LORD who spoke to her: "You are the God who sees me," for she said, "I have now seen the One who sees me.""

In Genesis 48, when Jacob is looking back on his whole life and finally accepting his name "Israel" he blesses two grandsons with these words from Genesis 48:14-16:

"May the God before whom my fathers Abraham and Isaac walked faithfully, the God who has been my shepherd all my life to this day, the Angel who has delivered me from all harm — may He bless these boys. May they be called by my name and the names of my fathers Abraham and Isaac, and may they increase greatly on the earth."

THE APPEARING OF GOD

Novatian (200-258 AD), writing "On the Trinity" says, in chapter 18:

"Moses tells us... that "God was seen of Abraham." And yet the same Moses hears from God, that "no man can see God and live." If God cannot be seen, how was God seen? Or if He was seen, how is it that He cannot be seen? For John also says, "No man hath seen God at any time;" and the Apostle Paul, "Whom no man hath seen, nor can see." But certainly the Scripture does not lie; therefore, truly, God was seen. Whence it may be understood that it was not the Father who was seen, seeing that He never was seen; but the Son, who has both been accustomed to descend, and to be seen because He has descended. For He is the image of the invisible God...

Wherefore it is the Son who is seen; but the Son of God is the Word of God: and the Word of God was made flesh, and dwelt among us; and this is Christ. What in the world is the reason that we should hesitate to call Him God, who in so many ways is acknowledged to be proved God?

And if, moreover, the angel meets with Hagar, Sarah's maid... Scripture sets forth this Angel as both Lord and God—for He would not have promised the blessing of seed unless the angel had also been God. Let them ask what the heretics can make of this present passage. Was that the Father that was seen by Hagar or not? For He is declared to be God.

But far be it from us to call God the Father an angel, lest He should be subordinate to another whose angel He would be.

But they will say that it was an angel. How then shall He be an angel if He be called God? This name is nowhere conceded to angels... we ought to understand it to have been God the Son, who, because He is of God, is rightly called God, because He is the Son of God. But, because He is subjected to the Father, and the Announcer of the Father's will, He is declared to be the Angel of Great Counsel.

Therefore, although this passage neither is suited to the person of the Father, lest He should be called an angel, nor to the person of an angel, lest he should be called God; yet it is suited to the person of Christ that He should be both God because He is the Son of God, and should be an angel because He is the Announcer of the Father's mind...

There can be no doubt but that it was He who was the guest of Abraham on the destruction of the people of Sodom, it is declared: "Then the Lord rained upon Sodom and upon Gomorrah fire and brimstone from the Lord out of heaven."...the Lord rained fire from the Lord... And this is the Word of God. And the Word of God was made flesh, and dwelt among us; and this is Christ. It was not the Father, then, who was a guest with Abraham, but Christ. Nor was it the Father who was seen then, but the Son; and Christ was seen...

Moreover, says the Scripture, the same Angel and God visits and consoles the same Hagar when driven with her son from the dwelling of Abraham."

It really does seem that Jacob understood that Divine Angel to be the God of Abraham, Isaac and Jacob. Another powerful example happens in Exodus 3:2-6.

The angel of the LORD appeared to (Moses) in flames of fire from within a bush. Moses saw that though the bush was on fire it did not burn up. So Moses thought, "I will go over and see this strange sight—why the bush does not burn up." When the LORD saw that he had gone over to look, God called to him from within the bush, "Moses! Moses!" And Moses said, "Here I am." "Do not come any closer," God said. "Take off your sandals, for the place where you are standing is holy ground." Then he said, "I am the God of your father, the God of Abraham, the God of Isaac and the God of Jacob." At this, Moses hid his face, because he was afraid to look at God.

Again, it is hard to read this without concluding that the Angel of the LORD is truly the LORD God of Abraham, Isaac and Jacob.

The word "Angel" simply means "one who is sent" or "messenger". There are hundreds of millions of angelic **creatures** who are sent to do the will of the Living God, but Jesus is no creature! He is The One sent to do the Father's will, and He rejoices in such a mission. It is His food and drink to do the Father's will.

In John 8:56-59 Jesus claimed that Abraham looked forward to meeting Him and when he did meet Jesus Abraham was overjoyed about it. This is most likely referring to the meeting at the beginning of Genesis 18 when Abraham was excited about the Lord God visiting with two angels. However, the religious people listening to Jesus in John 8 thought His claim was ridiculous.

"You are not yet fifty years old," they said to him, "and you have seen Abraham!"

Jesus would have to have been 2000 years old to have met Abraham – but He didn't even look 50!

Yet, instead of backing down from His claim Jesus said that before Abraham ever existed He is the "I Am" of Exodus chapter 3:14. His religious opponents knew exactly what He was saying: He was claiming to be the very One who met Moses at the burning bush.

Foundations

Day 20: The Law is all about Jesus

FRAMEWORKS

We have seen that Moses seems to hold the Trinitarian faith centred on Jesus, but now we want to spend a couple of studies seeing how the Law in particular is all about Jesus.

First we could note what the apostle Paul says about the Law in Romans 10:6-9. Before you read this, first read **Deuteronomy 30:11-16**, because Paul will not only quote from it but actually explain it line by line.

The righteousness that is by faith says: "Do not say in your heart, 'Who will ascend into heaven?'" (that is, to bring Christ down) or 'Who will descend into the deep?'" (that is, to bring Christ up from the dead). But what does it say? "The word is near you; it is in your mouth and in your heart," that is, the message concerning faith that we proclaim: If you declare with your mouth, "Jesus is Lord," and believe in your heart that God raised Him from the dead, you will be saved.

Paul literally believes that the message of Deuteronomy 30:11-16 is the very same message that he is preaching, that Jesus is LORD and God raised Him from the dead.

The thing that people often forget is that the ancient Law is all about grace and forgiveness. People sometimes think that the Law was about demanding moral perfection and absolute holiness, but most of the Law is actually dealing with grace, forgiveness and cleansing. Most of the Laws are displaying how the LORD God freely gives forgiveness and cleansing through His Eternal Son, the Great High Priest.

All the sacrifices and offerings are about cleaning and forgiving sinful and broken people. Obeying the Law actually required the ancient Church to make sacrifices for sin! It required a Day of Atonement to take away all the sin and uncleanness from the people and the Tabernacle itself.

CYPRIAN OF CARTHAGE ON JESUS AS THE LAMB

We heard from Novatian, a fiery North African who was excommunicated because he rejected anyone who had denied Jesus in the persecutions. A contemporary of his, who took a more gracious view of those who denied Jesus under torture, was Cyprian of Carthage (200-258).

In this quotation notice how easily he collects together different Scriptures and assumes they are all self-evidently speaking directly about Jesus. This is a short chapter from his second book of Testimonies.

THAT CHRIST IS CALLED A SHEEP AND A LAMB WHO WAS TO BE SLAIN AND CONCERNING THE MYSTERY OF THE PASSION.

In Isaiah: "He was led as a sheep to the slaughter, and as a lamb before his shearer is dumb, so He opened not His mouth. In His humiliation His judgment was taken away: who shall relate His nativity? ... His soul was delivered up to death, and He was counted among transgressors. And He bare the sins of many and was delivered for their offences."

Also in Jeremiah: "Lord, give me knowledge, and I shall know it: then I saw their meditations. I was led like a lamb without malice to the slaughter; against me they devised a device, saying, Come... let us erase His life from the earth, and His name shall no more be a remembrance."

Also in Exodus God said to Moses: "Let them take to themselves each man a sheep, through the houses of the tribes, a sheep without blemish, perfect, male, of a year old it shall be to you. You shall take it from the lambs and from the goats, and all the congregation of the synagogue of the children of Israel shall kill it in the evening; and they shall take of its blood, and shall place it upon the two posts, and upon the threshold in the houses, in the very houses in which they shall eat it... you shall not break a bone of it. But what of it shall be left to the morning shall be burnt with fire. But thus you shall eat it; dressed and ready, your sandals on your feet, and your staff in your hands; and you shall eat it in haste: for it is the Lord's Passover."

Also in the book of Revelation: "And I saw in the midst of the throne, and of the four living creatures, and in the midst of the elders, a Lamb standing as if slain, having seven horns and seven eyes, which are the seven spirits of God sent forth throughout all the earth. And He came and took the book from the right hand of God, who sat on the throne... and they sang a new song, saying, Worthy art Thou, O Lord, to take the book, and to open its seals: for Thou wast slain, and hast redeemed us with Thy blood from every tribe, and tongue, and people, and nation..."

Also in the Gospel: "On the next day John saw Jesus coming to him, and saith, Behold the Lamb of God, and behold Him that taketh away the sins of the world!"

The very fact that the sacrifices were constantly repeated was constantly reminding the people that the blood of mere animals cannot take away sin: only the Divine blood of the Lamb of God can do that (Heb 10:1-7).

Consider even the layout of the camp of the ancient Church centred on the Tent of Meeting, the Tabernacle.

> Read Numbers 2 carefully, but while you are reading it draw out a plan of what you are reading on a blank piece of paper.
>
> For example, in verse 3 we see that the tribe of Judah were furthest to the east, where the sun would rise. This is important because the Messiah would come from the tribe of Judah and so the whole camp would see the sun rising out of the tribe of Judah every day!
>
> Next to them, coming in towards the centre, was the tribe of Issachar and the finally on the eastern wing the tribe of Zebulun was closest in to the Tabernacle, which was at the very centre.
>
> CHALLENGE: note down the number of men in each of the collective wings – (186,400 for this eastern arm of the camp) – and try to make the different arms a proportionate length (so make the western arm shortest, and so on).
>
> When you have finished, with the proportionate lengths of each arm, what do you see?

It might feel impossible and ridiculous to the modern mind to think that the most ancient Church community in 1500 BC was consciously aware of the Trinity, Christ the Eternal Son, the Cross and Resurrection, the Sacraments of the Church, the Day of Judgement and a Resurrection future.

However, we are not dealing with the tiny possibilities of modern human beings here! We are dealing with the Infinite and Eternal God who walks through history in mystery and wonder.

Just imagine for a moment that the New Testament quotations of the Old Testament were all literally true and the early and medieval Church leaders were basically right in their handling of the Bible!

Foundations

Day 21: Jesus is the Great High Priest

FRAMEWORKS

The fact that Jesus is the Great High Priest of the heavens and the earth is shown most clearly in the Law of Moses.

We have already seen something of His great role as the one Mediator in the creation of the universe: all things were created in Him and through Him. We have seen how He is the One who makes the Unseen Father visible to His people. However, when we get to the very heart of the system of Law centred on the Tabernacle, we see that the focus of it all is the high priest.

Aaron was anointed as the first high priest. The process is described in Exodus 30:22-38.

> Take some time to consider how the special anointing oil was made. How much had to be made for the anointing of the high priest? Fill a bucket, if you can, with that quantity of water to see how much it is.
>
> Imagine the amazing smell of this oil. It could never be made for any other purpose (verse 32). What did anointing oil symbolise? See 1 Samuel 16:13 for a big clue!
>
> Read Numbers 17 to get a sense of the unlimited life in the high priest, to even give life to what is dead.

When Samuel anointed Saul (1 Samuel 10:1) he used a flask of oil and when he anointed David as king, he used a horn of oil (1 Samuel 16:1). How much oil is in a horn compared to the amount used for the high priest? If you had seen a king anointed and also a high priest anointed… who would you think of when you thought about "anointing"?

The point is this: the main title of Jesus is "Christ" or "Messiah" meaning "The Anointed One". To the ancient Church in the Old Testament that word "Messiah" was primarily associated with the high priest, rather than the king or a prophet (who also was anointed).

OUR DIVINE, COMPASSIONATE HIGH PRIEST

Charles Haddon Spurgeon preached a powerful sermon on Hebrews 5:2.

THE High Priest looked Godward and, therefore, he had need to be holy, for he had to deal with things pertaining to God.

But at the same time he looked manward—it was for men that he was ordained—that, through him, they might deal with God and, therefore, he had need to be tender.

It was necessary that he should be one who could have sympathy with men, otherwise, even if he could succeed Godward, he would fail to be a link between God and man from lack of tenderness and sympathy with those whom he sought to bring near to Jehovah.

Hence, the High Priest was taken from among men that he might be their fellow and have a fellow-feeling with them.

No angel entered into the holy place.
No angel wore the white garments.
No angel put on the ephod and the breastplate with the precious stones.

It was a man, ordained of God, who for his brothers, pleaded in the Presence of the Shekinah.

Many of us, I trust, have a desire within our hearts to come to God, but we need a High Priest.

But we need a High Priest, in order that we may draw near, who shall be a Man as well as God!

We may reflect with joy upon the Godhead of our great High Priest.

Inasmuch as it is His right, He counts it not robbery to be equal with God, but He communes with the Father as One that was by Him, as One brought up with Him, who was daily His delight, rejoicing always before Him.

But we ought, also, to be very grateful that we can come into touch with our High Priest on His human side and rejoice that He is truly Man.

For thus says the Lord, "I have laid help upon One that is mighty: I have exalted One chosen out of the people."

He is anointed, it is true, with the oil of gladness above His fellows, but still, He and they are one, "for which cause He is not ashamed to call them brethren."

...The High Priest of old was compassed with infirmities, but this was part of his qualification. "Yes," says one, "but he was compassed with sinful infirmities. But our Lord Jesus had no sin."

That is quite true, but please remember that this does not make Christ less tender, but more so.

Anything that is sinful, hardens – and inasmuch as He was without sin – He was without the hardening influence that sin would bring to bear upon a man!

He was all the more tender when compassed with infirmities, because sin was excluded from the list.

Jesus is the Divine Prophet, King and Priest – but it is the priestly work that lies at the very centre of His work and glory. The Cross is His great glory.

Now, the uniform worn by Aaron was almost like a "super hero costume"! When children put on such a costume they act almost as if they had super powers! When Aaron put on the high priest uniform, his clothes were showing off the powers and glory of the ultimate hero, the LORD Jesus Christ, the Divine High Priest over all creation. As high priest he was able to stand against the plague of death and everyone who sheltered behind him was safe – Numbers 16:44-50. In Exodus 28 we see his uniform described. Let's pick out four features.

1. **The Ephod (Exodus 28:6-14).** This apron had stones with the names of all the tribes inscribed upon them, showing how Christ Jesus carries His people into the Most Holy Place. Just as a fireman rescues incapacitated people by carrying them over his shoulder, so in all our weakness and deathly sickness of sin, our Divine High Priest has shoulders strong enough to carry us all.

2. **The Breast plate (Exodus 28:15-30).** This golden chest piece was covered in twelve precious stones, each one representing one of the twelve groups of the ancient Church. This showed how precious the people are to Christ and that He carried us over His heart.

3. **The Robe (Exodus 28:31-35).** The key feature was the hem, which had bells and pomegranates sewed on. Bells give their bright clear sound of victory, a small version of the clashing cymbals of Psalm 150:5! Even when the high priest was in the Most Holy Place the church family could hear him moving and know that he represented them there. Pomegranates are full of so many seeds – and in Numbers 20:5; Deuteronomy 8:8 and throughout the Song of Songs – pomegranates are a symbol of fertility and life. Christ our heavenly High Priest is full of victory and life!

4. **The Turban (Exodus 28:36-38).** The priest's turban had a plate of pure gold attached to the front and on it was written the following words: HOLY TO THE LORD. The priest was utterly dedicated to his job. Although all the earthly priests were sinful people, yet this golden sign was declaring that Jesus Christ is absolutely holy.

Foundations

Day 22: Jesus is the One Mediator

FRAMEWORKS

What is a mediator? What is mediation?

The Oxford English dictionary gives us the following definitions.

Mediator – "A person who attempts to make people involved in a conflict come to an agreement; a go-between."

Mediation – "Intervention in a dispute in order to resolve it; arbitration."

When Jesus was the one through whom all things were created, He was not involved in a conflict as such... even though He was bringing order to chaos and light into darkness. Nevertheless, even then He was the go-between: The One who took the will and designs of the Father and made them visible in the heavens and the earth.

After the sin of Adam & Eve it is much clearer to see how He is intervening "in a dispute", to put it mildly! He is always the One that the Father sends to reveal and redeem, in the power of the Spirit.

What about all the Levitical priests that surrounded the high priest?

Weren't they also doing this work of mediation?

When people are not used to reading the Old Testament carefully they assume that there were many priests who were all able to do this job of mediation. The idea is that the high priest was something like a boss who was in charge of all the priests, but basically all of them did the same job.

However, the truth is very, very different.

THE ONE MEDIATOR

Dr Martyn Lloyd-Jones preached on Ephesians 2:16:

"...there is only one way to be reconciled with God, namely, through Jesus Christ and Him crucified.

There is no access into the presence of God except through the one and only Mediator; 'that He might reconcile both in one body', and it is the only body, the only way.

It is in this one body, the Church; and no man ever has been or ever will be reconciled to God save in this way.

Abraham and the Old Testament saints, all whose sins had been covered, are really reconciled to God in Christ.

All in all future ages will be reconciled in the same way. It is by the grace of God and that alone that any man can be saved.

So I go on to the next principle, which I put like this. The reconciliation is achieved and produced by the Lord Jesus Christ.

'And that He'— He, the Lord Jesus—'might reconcile both unto God in one body'. He! Oh that we all might be clear about this! There is no hope for man apart from Him.

He came into the world because it was the only way. No man, I say again, ever can or ever will save himself by his own efforts or striving, no matter what is preached to him.

Neither can the law save him; as Paul says:

'What the law could not do in that it was weak through the flesh ...'.

Christ had to come.

'God was in Christ reconciling the world unto Himself', and there is no other way.

Here the apostle puts the emphasis upon the Lord Jesus Christ.

It was God who sent Him, but it was Christ by coming and by all His active and passive obedience who has done it.

'He is our peace', and He alone is our peace. I say again that unless we ascribe all the praise and the honour and the glory to the Lord Jesus Christ we are not Christians.

It is His action; it is God's action in and through Him. Man is dead in trespasses and sins, he is an enemy and alien in his mind by wicked works, he is a God–hater, he does nothing and can do nothing good.

How is reconciliation possible? We found the answer in the definition of the word: it is an action from above, it is a move on God's part, the God against whom we have rebelled and on whom we have turned our backs... It is all in Jesus Christ. It is all the grace of God in Christ. 'God was in Christ, reconciling the world unto Himself.' That is the message."

There was only one high priest – and that high priest was the only one who was ever able to go into the Most Holy Place, which represented the highest heaven where the Father sits enthroned.

> Read Leviticus 16:1-17.
>
> What details stand out for you?
> What did Aaron have to do when he did go behind the curtain into the Most Holy Place? Why?
> We will examine this Day of Atonement in more detail in a future module.

The thousands of Levitical priests were all appointed to **assist** the high priest. Notice all the instructions given to them in Numbers 3:5-39. Each of the three family divisions with the tribe of Levi were given specific duties for the care and transportation of the Tabernacle. In Deuteronomy 33:10 we see that they were also to teach the Law to the whole ancient Church.

However, none of them were ever allowed to come into the Most Holy Place where the LORD was enthroned between the cherubim.

Let that sink in for a moment: only the high priest could ever symbolically "enter into heaven" – and then only on one day a year.

None of the other Levitical "priests" were ever able to mediate between heaven and earth, even in this earthly **model** of the heavenly reality.

In the Law written down by Moses, there was only one mediator – Aaron, the high priest.

1 Timothy 2:5 says "there is one God and One Mediator between God and humanity, the man Christ Jesus."

How does Paul know this and how can he assert it with such confidence? The whole system of Law under Moses, given by the LORD God, was centred on this very truth.

Just as there was only one mediator in the tabernacle that represented the heavens and the earth, so in the divine reality there is only One Mediator, Jesus Christ Himself.

He alone is the Great High Priest over the whole creation and humanity.

Foundations

Day 23: Jesus and the gods

FRAMEWORKS

Jesus of Nazareth dismisses all the gods in the world.

The Bible shows us many conflicts between the different gods of the world and the One God who is Father, Son and Holy Spirit... and in every single one of these contests, the Father, Son and Holy Spirit win in spectacular and conclusive ways.

The "gods" are angelic powers that have fallen and rebelled against the Living God who created them in the beginning. Corrupted and proud, they try to take the place of the LORD God and deceive the world. Every god that stands in the way of the Biblical God is humiliated and shown to be false.

> Read 1 Samuel 5:1-5 for one of these confrontations. Then try to read Isaiah 36-37 for an amazing display of the Angel of the LORD.

The LORD had to humiliate the god Dagon in his own temple in order to demonstrate to the world that He had total sovereignty over this false god. Dagon is nothing more than a creature who has rebelled against his Lord and Master.

Isaiah 36-37 is a wonderful story of the Angel of the LORD confronting the power of the "gods". It seemed that the world and evil was about to utterly triumph over the ancient church. The pagan commander literally mocked the LORD Jesus - and yet, when the church went to sleep one night, by the time morning had come, without any help or input from the church, the LORD Jesus defeated all their enemies. The story ends with the pagan gods unable to protect their king from even the threat of two murderers.

In Exodus 12:12 we see how the gods of Egypt were judged. After the crossing of the Red Sea, Moses sings a song of triumphant worship (Exodus 15:11):

"Who among the gods is like you, O LORD? Who is like you - majestic in holiness, awesome in glory, working wonders?"

Moses' father-in-law, Jethro, makes a wonderful speech

NO GOD BUT JESUS

The modern theologian Jurgen Moltmann brilliantly shows the stark choice between the Crucified God and the demonic gods of the world.

"Luther (once said): 'You might just as well pray to the devil if you have to have any God but Jesus.'

For the Christian there is no gradation between the crucified Jesus and the gods, as though God were less evident in the world, world history and world politics, and more evident in Christ.

This notion of a gradation between a natural theology and a Christian theology can easily be unmasked...

Between 'God in Christ' and the gods outside and in other representations there stands the cross of that God, and with it the alternative 'aut Christus—aut Caesar' – (either Christ or Caesar), just as Elijah once posed the alternatives 'either Yahweh or the Baals'.

Hence Luther and Zinzendorf did not speak of other gods or other revelations of the same God, but of 'God and non-God', of 'God and the devil'.

The cross of Jesus marks a divide between the human God (Jesus Christ) who is freedom and love and the 'counter-God' who keeps men under his sway and dominated by fear, like demons, and sucks them up into nothingness.

However, the 'crucified God' here cannot be interchanged with the 'God of Christians', for by the terms of a psychological or sociological analysis the God of the Christians is not always the 'crucified God'.

Only rarely is this the case.

Even for historical Christianity the cross, if it is understood radically and down to its final consequences, is a scandal and foolishness."

From the end of chapter 5 in The Crucified God.

The great preacher and Patriarch of Constantinople, John Chrysostom (349-407) preached on Ephesians 1:20-23:

"(The apostle) says not merely "above" but "far above."

For God is higher than the powers on high.

So He led Jesus up there, the very one who shared our lowly humanity.

He led him from the lowest depth to the highest sovereignty, beyond which there is no higher honour.

"Above every sovereignty," he says: not merely compared with this or that.... What gnats are compared with humans, so is the whole creation compared with God."

about all this in Exodus 18:9-11. After all this it is no surprise that the Ten Commandments begin in the way that they do (Exodus 20:1-3):

"And God spoke all these words: "I am the LORD your God, who brought you out of Egypt, out of the land of slavery. You shall have no other gods before me."

As soon as the Ten Commandments have been spoken, the Father again insists on His people rejecting all the gods in the world: "Then the LORD said to Moses, "Tell the Israelites this: `You have seen for yourselves that I have spoken to you from heaven: Do not make any gods to be alongside me; do not make for yourselves gods of silver or gods of gold."

In Exodus 23 this becomes an insistent and constant message:

**verse 13: "Do not invoke the names of other gods; do not let them be heard on your lips".
verse 23-4: "My Angel will go ahead of you... Do not bow down before their gods or worship them or follow their practices. You must demolish them and break their sacred stones to pieces."
verse 31-33: "Do not make a covenant with them or with their gods. Do not let them live in your land, or they will cause you to sin against me, because the worship of their gods will certainly be a snare to you."**

One of the biggest challenges to our theological foundations in this age is the modern Western idea of the world religions. Most of the Christians in the world have always lived as a small minority surrounded by powerful religions. All their theology and culture has developed with this awareness. However, Western theology has had a long history of "Christendom", where churches dominated the entire continent of Europe. Therefore, when they began to explore the world and discover that there were vast, ancient and diverse religions all over the world, it created quite a crisis for Europeans who had never thought about this before! At an international theological "workshop", one of the questions set by a European was "how are we to understand the challenge of other religions?". All the African and Asian theologians in the room were genuinely completely puzzled: they knew nothing else than this profound conflict with religions. Why didn't the Europeans understand how to deal with this?

Foundations

Day 24: More on Jesus and the gods

FRAMEWORKS

The New Living Translation presents Ephesians 2:1-2 like this: "Once you were dead because of your disobedience and your many sins. You used to live in sin, just like the rest of the world, obeying the devil—the commander of the powers in the unseen world. He is the spirit at work in the hearts of those who refuse to obey God."

As we establish our deep theological foundations, we cannot be ignorant or naïve about the spiritual powers and the spiritual warfare that is constantly going on. As soon as we preach Jesus Christ, the powers of this present darkness will attack us and try to prevent us. We defeat them not by trying to be "ghostbusters", but by planting churches and training people to be disciples of Jesus. His Name is far above all the powers and principalities of this age.

> Read Ephesians 1:18-23 and genuinely pray that your eyes will be enlightened to see the incomparably great power of Christ over all the powers, "gods" and dominions of this present age.

The book of Deuteronomy makes even more of this important truth. The constant temptation is to follow the gods of the world, whether they are sophisticated intellectual gods or crass, wooden idols. The constant yearning of the **sinful** human heart is to turn away from the **Living** God and go after the dead idols and false gods.

Deut 32:15-18 - "Jeshurun grew fat and kicked; filled with food, he became heavy and sleek. He abandoned the God who made him and rejected the Rock his Saviour. They made Him jealous with their foreign gods and angered Him with their detestable idols. **They sacrificed to demons, which are not God-- gods they had not known, gods that recently appeared, gods your fathers did not fear**. You deserted the Rock, who fathered you; you forgot the God who gave you birth. The LORD saw this and rejected them because He was angered by his sons and daughters".

EPHESIANS 1:21

Dr Martyn Lloyd-Jones preached on this amazing verse.

"(The apostle Paul) continues with his description of the glory and honour given to the Son.

God has 'set Him at His own right hand in the heavenlies, far above all principality and power and dominion and every name that is named, not only in this world but also in that which is to come'.

The learned commentators, as is their way, when they come to this passage, spend much time in trying to work out to whom these terms 'power' and 'principality' and 'dominion' refer. Was the Apostle thinking of evil angels or of good angels? That is the question which they discuss.

What is surely quite clear is that Christ has been placed in a position of authority and honour which is above **all** powers.

There are evil powers which have exercised dominion in this world - 'We wrestle not against flesh and blood, but against principalities, against powers, against the rulers of the darkness of this world, against spiritual wickedness in the heavenlies' (Ephesians 6:12).

The world is as it is today because of these principalities and powers, these unseen spiritual forces.

But the Son of God is far above them all. He is greater than they in might and dignity and majesty and position.

But I maintain that the Apostle refers not only to such powers but also to the good angels, the blessed angels.

He has been set above them all.

A perfect description of this is found in the first chapter of the Epistle to the Hebrews, where the author describes something of the greatness of the angels and their power, and then ends by saying that, after all, they are but 'ministering spirits' (v. 14).

They are not equal to the Son; they lack His uniqueness. God has not said to any of them, 'Thou art my Son, this day have I begotten thee' (Hebrews 1:5). Such language is reserved only for His own Son.

I suggest, therefore, that the Apostle is telling us that the Son of God, our Lord Jesus Christ, is elevated and exalted even above the archangels Gabriel and Michael, the special servants of God.

He is above them all, He is at God's right hand, sharing the throne with His Father, far above all principality and might and dominion and power.

Such is the measure of the power of God as displayed in the Lord Jesus Christ. The Father not only raised Him from death and the grave but He has elevated Him and placed Him in the place of supreme honour and authority at His own right hand."

Notice how Moses identifies the gods as 'demons'. They are real creatures who have tried to take the place of the True God in the hearts and minds of their followers. Following a god other than the Trinity is not just an intellectual curiosity... it is the worship of demons.

This is important for us to hold in mind as we study the different religions of the world. People may have answered prayers and miracles; they may experience powers and dreams; they may enjoy healing and insight, all from their 'god' or 'gods'.

If we assume that all the gods are imaginary, we will have a real crisis when we face such "supernatural" occurrences. Moses equips us for the real world, telling us that the gods are demons, and they are obviously not God because they have 'recently appeared'.

As the Maker of the heavens, the Trinity is, naturally, the Maker of the "gods".

Psalm 86:8-10 - "Among the gods there is none like you, O Lord; no deeds can compare with yours. All the nations you have made will come and worship before you, O Lord; they will bring glory to your name. For you are great and do marvellous deeds; you alone are God."

The Living God has a total sovereignty over all the angels, even over those that have rebelled against Him. The other gods must actually bow before the Father, Son and Holy Spirit.

Psalm 82:1 - "God presides in the great assembly; He gives judgement among the gods:"
Psalm 95:3 - "The LORD is the great God, the great King above all gods."
Psalm 135:5-6 - "I know that the LORD is great, that our Lord is greater than all gods. The LORD does whatever pleases Him, in the heavens and on the earth, in the seas and all their depths."

In fact, Psalm 97 goes further and begins to call on the gods to repent of their rebellion and begin to join the Church in the true worship of God the Father.

Psalm 97:7-9 - "All who worship images are put to shame, those who boast in idols - worship Him, all you gods! Zion hears and rejoices and the villages of Judah are glad because of your judgements, O LORD. For you, O LORD, are the Most High over all the earth; you are exalted far above all gods."

Foundations

Day 25: The universe proclaims Jesus

FRAMEWORKS

Can we get a general knowledge of God without Jesus Christ simply by looking at the natural world around us? Doesn't creation speak about God without the need for Jesus?

Some have claimed that Romans 1:18-20 suggests that creation gives "general truths" about God that anybody can know but not the truth in Christ and the gospel. One way of putting it is that there is a general knowledge of God in creation and a **saving** knowledge of God in Church.

However, what would be the purpose of a knowledge of God in creation that isn't accurate, that excludes the very heart and essence of who God is?
Is the witness of nature a Unitarian witness?
If the creation does not speak of Jesus Christ or the Trinity, why doesn't it? Is the creation a heretic?
Why wouldn't He tell the truth about Himself in creation?
Why would He say one thing in creation but a very different thing in the events and words in the Bible?

To put it bluntly - what is the point of God revealing Himself in creation if this knowledge is useless? If this "general knowledge of God" cannot possibly save a person what is the point of this "general revelation"? Even if a person pays faithful attention to this "non-saving knowledge of God", it can't do them any good. Why would the LORD Jesus be revealing Himself in a useless way?

If the general revelation of God says nothing about Jesus Christ then a non-Christian person has a pretty good excuse when they face Christ on Judgement Day - they can simply look Him in the eye and say, "Well, who are you supposed to be? The creation didn't say anything about you."

Now, if God has made such a non-Christological revelation of Himself, don't the followers of other religions follow it faithfully? If the revelation of God in nature is just of some kind of undefined 'one god' who is powerful and wise, then the Muslims definitely follow it.

WHY DON'T PEOPLE HEAR THE SERMON OF CREATION?

The most stark and wonderful statement about the sermon of creation can be found in Colossians 1:23. Every creature in the universe has heard the gospel! The creation does nothing less than preach the very same gospel that the apostle Paul preached to the Colossians.

A 20th century theologian said:

The first article of the Creed concerning God the Father and His work (of creation) is not a sort of 'forecourt' for the Gentiles, a realm in which Christians and Jews and Gentiles, believers and unbelievers are next to each other in the presence of something about which there might be some measure of agreement in describing it as the work of God the Creator... We are not nearer to believing in God the Creator, than we are to believing that Jesus Christ was conceived by the Holy Spirit and born of the Virgin Mary. It is not the case that the truth about God the Creator is directly accessible to us and that only the truth of the second article needs a revelation.

Our understanding of Jesus Christ needs to be very big to cope with the Bible's presentation of Him. He is not just God's best word to us - He is God's only Word. The creation speaks of Him, because it is through Him that it was all created, and it is by Him that it is all sustained (Colossians 1:15-17). There can be no excuse for any human failing to trust in Him.

The fact that sinful human beings never arrive at these conclusions based on their own observations of the world is exactly Paul's conclusion in Romans chapters 1-3.

Although the human race **did** originally know God (in the Garden of Eden), now the human race is blinded by wickedness and hides the truth of God, suppressing the truth in unrighteousness.

Nobody knows the Living God until they are saved - until their eyes are opened. Creation proclaims Christ, but it doesn't bring people to follow Jesus. Why not? Because of the sinfulness in the hearts and minds of humanity - Romans 1:18-19; Genesis 6:5; Jeremiah 17:9.

In Psalm 19 even though the creation preaches Christ, yet it is only through the Bible & Church that understanding, wisdom and salvation come.
Why? Because Romans 1:16 it is through the mission of the Church that God exercises His power for salvation. As it is stated in Ephesians 3:10, God wishes to display His manifold wisdom through the Church. So, although the creation preaches the same message as the Church it is only through the Church that God exercises His power for salvation. God has decided to do all His mission through us, through the Church. We are His ambassadors.

Unless we serve Church life and take Church to the world, nobody will ever believe in Christ. Without the mission of the Christian Church, the world is (Ephesians 2:12) 'without hope and without God'. Without the Church's evangelism the world is doomed to go to Hell. Those without the gospel witness of Church cannot be saved.

It is true that the LORD Jesus sometimes sends dreams and visions to send people along to Church - and perhaps opens their eyes to aspects of the creation to drive them to Church, but always they can only come to know Jesus and find His rescue in the Church family.

As we have already considered all knowledge of God is through Jesus Christ - and the revelation through creation leaves humanity inexcusable when we all stand before Jesus Christ on Judgement Day, according to Romans 1:18-20. How will we be judged on that day? We will be condemned or declared righteous according to whether we have trusted Jesus Christ or not - John 16:7-9. Judgement Day has nothing to do with whether we have been moral, religiously well-intentioned, charitable or criminals. Sin is not defined by mere morality but by our love for and trust in Jesus, the Eternal Son who we were made for.

> Read Romans 10:9-18, then follow up Paul's quotation of verse 18 by reading the whole of Psalm 19.
>
> Is Jesus for everyone? Has everybody heard about Jesus? How does Paul know that everybody has heard the good news about Jesus?
>
> What is the prime example, in Psalm 19, of the creation proclaiming Jesus?

Maybe we have sung "Jesus is LORD, creation's voice proclaims it, for by His power each tree and flower was planned and made. Jesus is LORD! The universe declares it. Sun, moon and stars in heaven cry Jesus is LORD!"

There are many other songs that grasp this same truth: the waves, the trees, the animals and the weather all honour Jesus, the LORD of All, the One in whom they all hold together. Psalm 19 invites us to look at the sun rising in the east and instantly defeating the darkness of the night. This powerful witness seems to travel across the heavens giving light and life to everybody and everything on earth. This heavenly "bridegroom" shows the way to the west – which makes more sense if we think about Genesis 3:24 and 4:16.

To the eyes of faith, the eyes of those who have been switched on to reality, this daily cycle of the sun proclaims the character of Jesus Christ, the light of the world, the One in whom the whole creation holds together.

In Revelation 5:13 the apostle John is given ears to hear the glorious song of creation about which Psalm 19 was speaking: "Then I heard every creature in heaven and on earth and under the earth and on the sea, and all that is in them, singing: 'To Him who sits on the throne and to the Lamb be praise and honour and glory and power, forever and ever!'"

Foundations

Day 26: The meaning of the world

FRAMEWORKS

What is the meaning of the world? Or, to get specific, what is the meaning of a tree growing by your house or a flower in your garden or a cloud wandering overhead or a spider making a web in your bathroom?

The Victorians used to have a special meaning for all the different flowers, so you could send someone a very clear message by the flowers you sent them! Daisies meant innocence; daffodils meant chivalry; crocuses were youth; roses love and violets modesty. The system had complicated rules, but it was all invented by human beings. They didn't claim that the Living God created daffodils to communicate the virtue of chivalry.

So, why did the LORD God design daffodils? What is HIS meaning for daffodils? Does the world have any meaning at all? Do all the creatures have specific meaning and purpose? Is it possible to ask "why" questions about trees, oceans, flowers and planets that are real "why" questions about meaning, purpose, symbolism and theology? A child might ask why is the sky blue and get palmed off with an answer about atmosphere and sunlight, but that is not what the child is really asking: they want to know why the sunlight and the atmosphere has been designed to produce this specific kind of blue. What does the colour **blue** mean?

It is hard for modern people to even think of meaning in this way. A huge revolution in understanding the world happened throughout the past 500 years: the world began to be understood on the model of an impersonal, clockwork machine, without symbolic meaning and even the Bible was read in a flat way, taking away all the symbolic meaning and reducing it to bare historical accounts.

Think about the Lord's Supper. We eat bread and drink wine. We could analyse the chemical composition of the bread and wine or test them for nutritional value. However, none of that kind of analysis tells us anything of the meaning of this bread and wine, that when the Church gathers to eat this it is nothing less than a genuine encounter with Jesus Christ Himself, a "fellowship" in the very body and blood of Jesus Himself – 1 Corinthians 10:16.

KNOWING THE CREATOR

There used to be a series where the host would go around an anonymous celebrities house and based on the features that the camera suggestively lingered over, the identity of the owner had to be guessed.

Without knowing the owner all the different features might seem strange or odd, but when they were revealed at the end, all the different features made sense and we could all breath a kind of "aha" as we realised why they had that kind of furniture, with that wallpaper, with those paintings and with that kind of kitchen.

In that same way, the Eternal Word has designed and decorated the heavens and the earth in His own style, imprinted with His own character, as an expression of the invisible Father.

On their own, out of context [viewed from 'outside' as C. S. Lewis might say] all the details of creation are just an overwhelming collection of details. They can be related to each other to a degree so that we may build up something of an account of the mechanisms and structure of the whole, but the meaning and "authorial intent" of the decor is missed... UNLESS we know the 'celebrity owner' and have His own written account of His character and ways.

When we are in His Church and enjoying fellowship with Him, His world makes sense, not just in the big general features, but increasingly and gloriously in the details.

When we are members of His household then we constantly look about the 'house' and recognise all kinds of things as being "just like Him".

On the original series, after the secret identity is revealed, people would say things like "Oh, yes, it is just like her to have that kind of wallpaper and that rug in her bathroom" or "after what happened to him that year, we can see why he had that photo on the wall" etc.

In just this way, after we come to know the LORD Jesus Christ and as the spectacles of Scripture and Church give us better and better vision of reality, so we can begin to see the whole creation in that way - "oh, it is just like Jesus Christ to make the trees in that way and the stars like that" or "given what happened to Him, we can see why He designed seeds to be like that".

In other words, the non-Christian who does not know the LORD Jesus Christ or the Scriptures or Church of course cannot make any sense of all these things. They can appreciate something of the superficial structure and mechanisms of the heavens and the earth, but the significance and meaning seems arbitrary, ridiculous and unbelievable.

We were designed to know Him and we were created in the Garden of God in a gracious relationship of love and openness. The fact that we have lost this position is the reason that we no longer have that constant sense of "aha, it is so like Him to make moss, rocks, fish, birds, clouds, grass, arms, hair, water, gravity etc. etc. like that".

The physical analysis of a wedding ring will not tell us about the relationship of its owner. That ring is set within a covenant relationship – and in **that** relationship the meaning of the ring is very clear. So, all the wonders and details of the world begin to come into focus once we are in Church, in fellowship with the Designer, Creator and Sustainer of the whole creation.

Our ancient and medieval ancestors took it for granted that everything in the world "meant something" – even numbers had deep symbolic meaning. We of course see all this in the Bible. Jesus picks up a seed and explains how the seed is meant to make us think about His death and resurrection – John 12:24. Jesus rebukes a storm and curses a fig tree as if they were not fulfilling their true meaning and purpose. He tells us to learn from the birds who have such instinctive trust in their heavenly Father. The very earth quakes when He dies.

Think about the meaning seen in storms and weather, animals and birds, trees and flowers throughout the Bible, especially in the Psalms. Remember this is the Word of God not just human expressions of what these things "make them feel or think about".

> Read Proverbs 30:15-33 and chew over the lessons drawn from the natural world.
>
> Think of the trees clapping their hands in Isaiah 55:12. Is that how you see trees? When flowers lean towards the sun, what meaning can you see in that? When they have no light, what happens to them?

We might not see and understand the meaning of every aspect of creation. When Solomon was wise it is said he even understood the meaning of the moss or lichen growing on the walls – 1 Kings 4:33. The point is that we begin to see that everything has meaning. Most of us were constantly indoctrinated with the idea that there is no meaning in the universe other than what we create for ourselves. When our basic foundation in life reminds us that everything has meaning in the LORD Jesus Christ then everything looks very, very different. As George Wade Robinson would sing:

"Heaven above is softer blue, Earth around is sweeter green; Something lives in every hue Christless eyes have never seen: Birds with gladder songs o'erflow, Flow'rs with deeper beauties shine, Since I know, as now I know, I am His, and He is mine."

Foundations

Day 27: Church is where we meet Jesus

FRAMEWORKS

One of the terrible legacies of some aspects of 19th century theology was to imagine serious, rigorous theology could be done outside of a local Church family.

Church is where we meet Jesus.

If Jesus is the central block in our Foundations, then we need to meet with Him and share life with Him. The last words that Jesus spoke to us as He ascended up into heaven are found in Matthew 28:18-20:

"All authority in heaven and on earth has been given to me. Therefore, go and make disciples of all nations, baptizing them in the name of the Father and of the Son and of the Holy Spirit, and teaching them to obey everything I have commanded you. And surely, I am with you always, to the very end of the age."

When Jesus ascended to the Father's throne He went with all authority, but what was this authority for? To go throughout the whole world discipling whole nations, but not in some abstract sense of sharing information but by baptising them into Church membership.

Since the 18th century there has been an ever-growing idea that mission is done **outside** of Church by organisations and agencies! How absurd! It is only through the Church with Word and Sacrament that sinful human beings can become disciples of the LORD Jesus Christ. It is in Church that we teach one another how to obey everything that Jesus commanded. It is in Church that He is with us to the very end of the age – through His Word and Sacraments, in our worship and life together.

Matthew 25 is a wonderful chapter about Church life: being always ready for His return (verses 1-13) and then how we are to use what He gives us in fruitful ways while we wait for His coming (verses 14-30). In Matthew 25:31-46 Jesus gives us a clear picture of how Church differs so completely from the world. The sheep in Church don't even notice how they are caring for one another, visiting each other in hospital or prison and in each case they are meeting with Jesus in their brothers and sisters.

EVERYTHING COMES TO US THROUGH CHURCH FROM CHRIST

Paul Bayne lived from 1573 – 1617. He was a powerful Puritan preacher who brought Richard Sibbes to Jesus. This is a taste of his explanation of Church from the end of Ephesians 1:20-21 –

"God placed all things under His feet and appointed Him to be head over everything for the church, which is His body, the fullness of Him who fills everything in every way."

"By being partakers of Christ Himself we come to be filled with the fulness of grace and glory in Him, as by eating and taking the substance of earthly nourishment we come to have the virtue in them. These benefits are conveyed to us by the means of grace, viz., the Word and the Sacraments...

The Church is His body"; the fulness of Him who filleth all in all." "The Church is His body"; then He is its Head: the Church is "His fulness," and "He filleth all in all."

Let us consider these weighty words.

1. The Lord Jesus Christ is the Head of His Church.

Like the head in our natural body, He is the channel of all their perceptions, the source of all their desires, the guide of all their actions.

Through Him they see and hear and think, by Him they live and move and have their being.

As our text says, "He filleth all in all"—every member with all its life.

2. The reality and intimacy of this union will be more fully realized if we observe, not only what the Lord Jesus Christ is to His disciples, but also what they are to Him. Paul tells us not only that the Lord Jesus Christ is the Head of the Church, but also that "the Church is His body"—not only that Christ "filleth all in all," but also that "the Church is His fulness."

The goats however, in the world, never cared for the Church (or for each other in a truly God-like way) and so when Jesus comes to embrace His Church and marry her forever, there is no place in that future for the goats. They are thrown out into the outer darkness. **If they did not have room for Jesus now in Church life, there will be no room for them in His future.**

Remember, all of humanity was designed to simply live Church life all day, every day. Church is not an addition to real life or a weekly duty. Church is how we live together all day, every day. Sometimes we gather together for worship, prayer, Word and Sacraments, but most of the time we disperse out into all our different walks of life – but always we are sharing life together, helping one another, encouraging one another, challenging each other when we fall.

Yes, we always confess our sins to one another, which can make us feel very vulnerable and ashamed, but when our sins are brought into the light within Christ's Body, His Church, then we have nothing to be afraid of. If God raised Jesus from the dead after He was so God-forsaken and cursed, then His blood can always make us clean. Church is where that blood is applied. Church is the very Body of Jesus – and the oil of the Spirit flows down from the Head, Jesus, down onto His Body – Psalm 133. We can only be filled with the Spirit in Church.

> Read Ephesians 4:17-32 carefully. See the contrast between the "Gentile" life outside of Church and the new life inside Church. Why does Paul write so much about thinking, understanding and minds? Why is it so important to control the focus of our minds?

Notice, especially, verse 21. Make sure you read in the old King James Version to see what it really says! In Church we can listen to Jesus Himself – not just words **about** Him.

We will have much more to say about Church in the Church series of Frameworks, but for now can we see that Church is where we meet Jesus? Anyone who claims to believe in Jesus but the centre of their life and mission is not their local Church is deluded and dangerous.

If we are going to grow in our knowledge of the Living God then we need to be within His Body, sharing life with His people, filled with His Spirit. If we are trying to do theology at arm's length, we will end up knowing nothing but empty words and human opinion.

Foundations

Day 28: Living the life of Jesus together in Church

FRAMEWORKS

In Genesis 6 when the LORD determined to bring a global flood on the earth, His place of safety was the mighty Ark, built by Noah over a hundred-year period. The LORD God did NOT issue individual life jackets to isolated individuals!

We cannot live the life of Jesus alone. We cannot taste eternal life as isolated individuals. The eternal life of God is a communal life, a family life.

Human schemes of self-improvement and meditation are all about individuals and isolation. Church is the very opposite: everything is about our shared life together. If we are going to build anything at all on the foundations, as Jesus said, we must obey His commandments – and those commandments are all in the context of Church.

Think of all the "one another" verses:

Romans 12:10 – "Be devoted to one another in love. Honour one another above yourselves." Then verse 16 – "Live in harmony with one another."
Romans 13:8 – "Let no debt remain outstanding, except the continuing debt to love one another."
Romans 14:13 – "Therefore let us stop passing judgment on one another."
Romans 15:7 – "Accept one another, then, just as Christ accepted you, in order to bring praise to God." Then verse 14, "You yourselves are full of goodness, filled with knowledge and competent to instruct one another."
Romans 16:6 – "Greet one another with a holy kiss."
1 Corinthians 1:10 – "...agree with one another in what you say and that there be no divisions among you, but that you be perfectly united in mind and thought."
2 Corinthians 13:11 – "Strive for full restoration, encourage one another, be of one mind, live in peace. And the God of love and peace will be with you."
Galatians 5:13 – "You, my brothers and sisters, were called to be free. But do not use your freedom to indulge the flesh; rather, serve one another humbly in love."
Ephesians 4:2 – "Be completely humble and gentle; be patient, bearing with one another in love."

MEMBERS OF HIS BODY TOGETHER

In the amazing commentary series *The Biblical Illustrator*, William Grant, commenting on Ephesians 1:21 says:

"Are we true members of the body of Christ?

Then let us realize that we have suffered and died with Him on Calvary.

Again, are we true members of the body of the Lord Jesus Christ?

Then we are delivered, not only from the punishment due to past, sins, but also from the power of present sinfulness.

Again, are we true members of the body of Christ?

Then let us remember that we are related, not only to Him, but also to one another as members of the same body.

Again, are we true members of the body of Christ?

Then we need not fear anything that man can do unto us. We cannot suffer but Jesus suffers with us. He is "afflicted in all our afflictions."

He would lose in our loss. He rejoices in our joy.

Once more, are we true members of the body of Christ?

Then our comfort reaches not only to the grave, but beyond it.

2. Of the duties which they owe to Him as the Head of government.

Obedience—implicit obedience—is the duty of each member of His body individually—obedience in all things.

I pass on to speak of the duty of the members of His body in their collective capacity—when associated together as churches.

The Lord Jesus Christ is the Head, not merely of each member of His body separately, but of "the whole body."

He has commanded His disciples to recognize each other, and to associate themselves together for common work and for common worship.

He has given rules for the government of His Church.

All these and such like commandments are addressed to the Church in its collective capacity."

Then verse 32 – "Be kind and compassionate to one another, forgiving each other, just as in Christ God forgave you." **Ephesians 5:19** – "Speaking to one another with psalms, hymns, and songs from the Spirit. Sing and make music from your heart to the Lord," Then verse 21 – "Submit to one another out of reverence for Christ."

This is vitally important. Trusting Jesus means loving His Church and serving His people. We show that we love Him when we keep His commandments – and these commandments are essentially "one another" commandments!

> Look up these verses to see the continuing pattern and see if you can pick out a favourite: Philippians 2:5; Colossians 3:13, 16; 1 Thessalonians 4:9, 18; 5:11; 2 Thessalonians 1:3; Hebrews 3:13; Hebrews 10:24-25; James 4:11, 5:9; 1 Peter 1:22; 3:8; 4:9; 5:5, 14; 1 John 3:11, 23; 4:7, 11-12; 2 John 1:5.

We need one another. The Spirit gives gifts to our local Church – 1 Corinthians 12:1-11. Each of us have some of what is needed, but only **together** do we have **all** that He is giving us.

Look at how the Apostolic churches lived together in Acts 2:42-47 and Acts 4:32-37. The Feast of Pentecost was the ancient festival of the full harvest, when there was plenty provided for the poor and needy. The full harvest of Christ's death and resurrection was shown on that day of Pentecost in Acts 2 when that local church shared life together in that full, wholehearted way.

If Church is a hobby for us or if there are other things that claim priority in our diaries, are we really connected to Christ the Head at all?

When any of us get distracted by side issues or start to puff ourselves up with what we know or what we are doing, we literally get disconnected from Jesus Christ!

Colossians 2:18-19 – "Such a person also goes into great detail about what they have seen; they are puffed up with idle notions by their unspiritual mind. They have lost connection with the Head, from whom the whole body, supported and held together by its ligaments and sinews, grows as God causes it to grow."

The reason for studying the Bible and theology is so that we may be more fruitful servants in Church life together, more able to obey the commands of Jesus.

Foundations

Day 29: Reading the Bible Together

FRAMEWORKS

The Bible was written by church leaders for churches and church members.

> Take time to look at the beginning of all Paul's letters. Who is he writing to and what for?
>
> Look at the letters that Jesus wrote in chapters 2-3 of Revelation. Who is He writing to?
>
> Finally, look at 2 Timothy 3:10-4:5 as Paul explains Church ministry to Timothy. What is the purpose of the Bible?

Think about the Old Testament books.

Moses was the leader of a huge Church family, the Church in the wilderness (Acts 7:38).
The Prophets were church preachers, preaching from Church to Church or else sent out by Church to plant Churches elsewhere, like Jonah.
The book of Psalms is a hymnbook for Church, not a general book of poetry!

Reading the Bible is not something for us to do all alone, but as a shared activity in Church. Paul told Timothy to make shared, public reading of the Bible a vital part of his Church life, 1 Timothy 4:13. "Until I come, devote yourself to the public reading of Scripture, to preaching and to teaching."

Paul assumes that reading the Bible is shared Church experience. The Holy Spirit gives gifts of teaching and understanding to the whole Church family, so we just can't understand it correctly all on our own.

We **should** read the Bible personally as well. It takes roughly 60 hours to read through the whole Bible. So if we read the Bible for half an hour in the morning and half an hour in the evening we should get through the Bible every two months – or 6 times a year.

READ THE BIBLE!

Spurgeon, once more, encourages to read the Bible seriously and extensively, in a sermon preached on January 15th 1865.

"*Search the Scriptures.*

Do not merely *read* them—search them; look out the parallel passages; collate them; try to get the meaning of the Spirit upon any one truth by looking to all the texts which refer to it.

Read the Bible consecutively: do not merely read a verse here and there—that is not fair.

You would never know anything about John Bunyan's Pilgrim's Progress if you opened it every morning and read six lines in any part and then shut it up again; you must read it all through if you want to know anything about it.

Get those books, say Mark or John; read Mark right through from beginning to end; do not stop with two or three verses, or a chapter, but try to know what Mark is aiming at.

It is not fair to Paul to take his epistle to the Romans and read one chapter: we are obliged to do it in public service; but if you want to get at Paul's meaning, read the whole epistle through as you would another letter.

Read the Bible in a commonsense way… Pray after you have read it as much as you like, but do not make a penance of what ought to be a pleasure.

...You have all some Christian friend who knows more than you do; go to them and try to get the thing explained.

Above all, when you have read any passage, and do understand it, **act it out**, and ask the Spirit of God to burn the meaning into your conscience till it is written on the fleshy tables of your heart."

In Book 4, chapter 26 of Ireneaus' book *Against Heresies*, he tells us how the Spirit provides teachers in Church so that we can understand it properly.

"Paul then, teaching us where one may find (faithful workers), says, "God has placed in the Church, first, apostles; secondly, prophets; thirdly, teachers."[6]

Where, therefore, the gifts of the Lord have been placed, there it is right for us to learn the truth, [namely,] from those who possess that succession of the Church which is from the apostles.

These faithful teachers are sound and blameless in conduct, as well as speaking in a pure and uncorrupted way.

For these (faithful workers) preserve this faith of ours in one God who created all things; and they increase that love [which we have] for the Son of God, who accomplished such marvelous things for our sake.

They expound the Scriptures to us without danger, neither blaspheming God, nor dishonouring the patriarchs, nor despising the rophets."

Remember the Bible is written in the simplest way possible: full of adventure, mystery, love, passion, philosophy, songs, inspiration, proverbs, letters, biographies, sermons and history. The longest chapter in the Bible is all about the Bible – Psalm 119 – and it relentlessly tells us how simple, clear and easy to understand the Bible is. It is a lamp so that even the simplest people can become wise.

Yet, in all our Bible reading, we always want to be grounded and centred on our shared Church life together. We need to make sure we listen to the Spirit-equipped teaching of our Church leaders with humility. We want to be teachable and eager to obey the Word of God.

In our experience it is excellent when churches pick one big book of the Bible or a couple of smaller ones each month, and then the whole Church family reads that together. Then at the end of the month the whole family can get together to share all they have learned. It is amazing how often the Holy Spirit puts the same verses and themes on many hearts throughout the Church family.

The Bible is easy to read together in this way, even with people who are brand new Christians, so long as we are asking the right questions as we read. We don't **need** encyclopaedias and big dictionaries. More than anything we need to ask the questions that the Bible expects us to ask – and then be ready to put it all into practice!

1. What did you learn about Jesus? (Luke 24:45-47)
2. What did you learn about yourself? (2 Timothy 3:16-17)
3. How were you corrected and challenged? (2 Timothy 3:16-17)
4. How do you feel you need to change to be a servant of God thoroughly equipped for every good work"? (2 Timothy 3:16-17)
5. What did you learn from the Scripture that will help you endure and be encouraged? (Romans 15:4)
6. What did you learn that will teach you to do works of service to build up your local Church? (Ephesians 4:11-16)
7. What have you learnt that helps you love the Lord your God with all your heart & with all your soul & with all your mind? (Matthew 22:37-40)
8. What has helped you love your neighbour as yourself? (Matthew 22:37-40)

Rev Steve Levy from Mount Pleasant Baptist Church in Swansea developed this way of Reading the Bible Together

Foundations

Day 30: The truth according to godliness

FRAMEWORKS

If we are going to build on the foundation of Christ and His Church then we need to realise that our knowledge of the truth is "according to godliness" as Titus 1:1 teaches.

The King James Version puts it like this "the acknowledging of the truth which is after godliness." Some translations suggests that the truth "leads to godliness", which is of course also true, but perhaps the truth in Titus 1:1 is different.

It is not just that the truth shows us how to live a godly life, but that a godly life enables us to understand the truth.

The truth that is in harmony with godliness has been in the plans and purposes of the Most Holy and Living God since before the world began.

> Read the whole book of Titus. It is just 3 short chapters and can be read in a few minutes. As you read it pay attention to the importance of lifestyle, behaviour and character.
>
> In the modern world a huge amount of the training of Church leaders is on intellectual qualities and academic qualifications. How would you describe the qualities that Paul describes to Titus as Titus was looking to appoint Cretan church leaders?

The truth of Jesus is "according to godliness". This not only means that it produces godliness but that if we are to truly understand this truth then we must be godly. Godliness is the mark of authentic truth – lifelong repentance from godlessness, a passion for serving in our local Church family, a constant turning **away from** the darkness and turning **towards** the light of Jesus.

The truth sets us free from darkness and sin... And also opens our eyes to see yet more truth.

False teaching comes from ungodliness and leads to ungodliness.

The truth of Jesus cannot just stay in our minds as some-

TRUTH AND GODLINESS TOGETHER

Richard Sibbes in his book *The Fountain Opened* writes:

"We may fetch a rule of discerning *when we are godly.*

What makes a true Christian? When he nakedly believes the grounds of divine truth, the articles of the faith, when he can patter them over—doth that make a true Christian? No.

But when these truths breed and work 'godliness.' For religion is a truth 'according to godliness,' not according to speculation only, and notion.

Wheresoever these fundamental truths are embraced, there is godliness with them; a man cannot embrace religion in truth, but he must be godly.

A man knows no more of Christ and divine things, than he values and esteems and affects and brings the whole inward man into a frame, to be like the things.

If these things work not godliness, a man hath but a human knowledge of divine things; if they carry not the soul to trust in God, to hope in God, to fear God, to embrace Him, to obey Him, that man is not yet a true Christian; for Christianity is not a naked knowledge of the truth, but godliness.

Religious evangelical truth is 'wisdom;' and wisdom is a knowledge of things directing to practice.

A man is a wise man, when he knows so as to practise what he knows. The gospel is a divine wisdom, teaching practice as well as knowledge.

It works godliness, or else a man hath but a human knowledge of divine things. Therefore, he that is godly, he believes aright and practiseth aright.

He that believes ill can never live well, for he hath no foundation. He makes an idol of some conceit he hath, besides the word; and he that lives ill, though he believe well, shall be damned too.

Therefore a Christian hath godly principles out of the gospel, and a godly carriage suitable to those principles.

And indeed, there is a force in the principles of godliness, from God's love in Christ, to stir up to godliness. The soul that apprehends God's truth aright cannot but be godly.

Can a man know God's love in Christ incarnate, and Christ's suffering for us, and His sitting at the right hand of God for us, the infinite love of God in Christ, and not be carried in affection back to God again, in love and joy and true affiance, and whatsoever makes up the respect of godliness?
It cannot be.

Therefore it is not a cold, naked apprehension, but a spiritual knowledge, when the soul is stirred up to a suitable disposition and carriage, that makes godliness."

thing interesting to think about or something comforting to believe. It is truth packed full with divine power and wisdom.

This is truth that changes lives.
This is truth that speaks of repentance and resurrection. This is truth that calls for obedience from beginning to end. This is truth that can only be understood when we obey. This is truth that is about transformation rather than merely information.

Such truth if believed and practised will make us Church servants of growing godliness. Our lives will be increasingly pleasing to God, increasingly centred on Jesus, increasingly useful to Him, and increasingly honouring to this Living God.

Godliness is not an optional luxury item in a theologian or Bible student. It is more necessary than anything else.

Holiness makes a Church family more and more beautiful with the beauty of God Himself. If godliness is the object of our desire, the word of God as a whole must increasingly be studied, known, believed, and lived out by us. We are sanctified through the truth.

The liberating truth of Jesus comes from the eternal truth and wisdom of the Living God – Titus 1:2. Jesus with His words and works is not just a random historical event in the middle of human history – verse 3.

Jesus of Nazareth is the Eternal Son of the Father – and everything He has done, from creating the universe, through to His birth, life, death, resurrection and ascension, were all planned before the universe began. When we are joined to Jesus through our local church we are joined to a way, truth and life that is older and deeper than the universe.

The life of God is the life of eternity. Just as the truth of Jesus began in eternity it leads on into eternity. **The only life that has any future is a Church life of truth and godliness.** There is no place in God's glorious creation for lies or ungodliness, or unbelief or sin.

The life of the ages, the eternal life of the Living God that was stored up in Jesus before the world began and poured out into Church, is our only hope.

Printed in Great Britain
by Amazon